101 ACTIVITIES FOR KIDS IN TIGHT SPACES

**CAROL STOCK
KRANOWITZ, M.A.**
Illustrations by Elaine Yabroudy

101 ACTIVITIES FOR KIDS IN TIGHT SPACES

At the Doctor's Office,
on Car, Train, and Plane Trips,
Home Sick in Bed . . .

ST. MARTIN'S GRIFFIN / NEW YORK
A SKYLIGHT PRESS BOOK

Published by arrangement with:
Skylight Press
260 West 72nd Street
Suite 6-C
New York, N.Y. 10023
(212) 874-4348

Design by Pei Loi Koay

Library of Congress Cataloging-in-Publication Data
Kranowitz, Carol Stock.
    101 activities for kids in tight spaces /
Carol Stock Kranowitz.
        p.   cm.
    ISBN 0-312-13420-7
    1. Play. 2. Parent and child. 3. Creative
activities and seatwork. 4. Personal space—
Psychological aspects. I. Title.
HQ782.K73 1995
649'.51—dc20   95-23753
                                           CIP

First Edition: December 1995
10 9 8 7 6 5 4 3 2 1

TO JEREMY AND DAVID

CONTENTS

"I'M ALL REVVED UP" or "I'M TOO POOPED TO PLAY " 95

MUSIC AND SOUND ACTIVITIES 110

"I FEEL YUCKY ALL OVER" 120
(S I C K I N B E D)

ACKNOWLEDGMENTS

MY PRIMARY thanks go to my father, Herman Stock, and to my late mother, Doris Stock; to my children, Jeremy and David; and to my sister, Ellen Stern, for their playful participation in most of these activities. I also thank my nieces, nephews, and students for joining in the fun.

I am grateful to many generous friends, all of whom are extraordinary teachers: Lynn Balzer-Martin, Julia Berry, Jane Healy, Peg Hoenack, Mike Kligerman, Mary Marcoux, Greg Myhr, George Petrides, Karen Strimple, Liz Wilson, and my colleagues at St. Columba's Nursery School in Washington, D.C.

In addition, I thank my husband, Alan, for his patience while I confined myself to the tight space in front of the word processor, as well as Lynn Sonberg and Meg Schneider of Skylight Press and Tina Y. Lee of St. Martin's Press for their editorial assistance.

INTRODUCTION

DEAR PARENT,

You were a kid once.

Do you remember how it felt to wait in the dentist's office for your name to be called? Do you remember long car trips over the river and through the woods to Grandmother's house, or, worse, long airplane rides? Do you remember rainy afternoons with nothing to do . . . and being confined to bed with the chicken pox . . . and having lots of energy to expend in a home that never had enough space?

Kids haven't changed. They will always want to burst out of tight spaces. They will always crave experiences like making mud pies, climbing apple trees, and riding bikes until dark. For our modern, urban, supervised children, however, such spontaneous activities are often out of the question.

When something of value is taken away, something of equal value must take its place. The trick is to find substitutes for old-fashioned activities that will fit kids' needs *and* fit into a tight space.

■ Helping Kids Get the Experiences They ■ Crave (But Can't Have)

What can you do to help kids get the experiences they crave?

1. First, understand that kids are born with an inner drive to learn. They learn through active participation in the world around them. An example of active participation is playing Ring Around the Rosy. The child who is in the play learns more and has more fun than the passive child who merely watches from the sidelines.

Active participation depends on children's ability to use *all* their senses—not only the familiar senses of vision and hearing, but also the senses that are less familiar because they are hidden inside our bodies. These "hidden" senses are:

- the tactile sense (through the skin), providing information about people and objects that we touch or that touch us;
- the vestibular sense (through the inner ear), telling us about our movement through space, our balance, and our resistance to the force of gravity; and
- the proprioceptive sense (through muscles and joints), informing us about our body position and what our bodies are doing.

Think of the child who plays Ring Around the Rosy. She is seeing, listening, holding other children's hands, moving in a circle, keeping her balance, purposely falling down, and scrambling up again. Touching and being touched, moving and being moved, she is using many senses simultaneously and effectively.

The efficient employment of all our senses is called "sensory integration." Sensory integration is the unconscious process of taking in sensory messages, analyzing them in the central nervous system, and organizing them for use, in order to function smoothly in daily life. To function smoothly—to become competent human beings—kids require a variety of active, multisensory experiences.

2. Second, unplug the TV and hide the videos. Television and videos provide passive entertainment and rob kids of the chance to learn through doing.

3. Third, use this book. *101 Activities for Kids in Tight Spaces* suggests activities that will satisfy kids' need to touch, move, play, and think. Some ideas are old standbys. Others I devised—sometimes in desperation and always in cramped quarters—while raising two exuberant boys, teaching hundreds of preschoolers, leading a den of Cub Scouts, organizing elementary school festivities, and running a birthday party business.

■ Helping Kids Choose an Activity ■

Kids who can read will be able to leaf through this book and make their own selections. Younger children, or those who are not self-starters, may need your suggestions, and for them it is often a good idea to offer two or three ideas.

You may be surprised by choices that children make. A child's interest in an activity may be affected by his or her internal personality traits, such as temperament, mood, learning style, perceptions, activity level, and attention span.

In addition, external factors, such as materials, place, weather, time of day, and company of an adult or friend will affect a kid's interest. It all depends.

Occasionally, your kid will choose an activity that just won't work at that particular moment—like Smash Hit Cookies when you are out of oatmeal. He may be unhappy or resentful, saying something like, "I never get to do anything I want to do!"

Turn this potentially tense moment into a teachable moment. First, respond sympathetically: "I know it seems unfair." Then, explain *briefly* why he can't do the desired activity: "We have no oatmeal." Then, ask for suggestions to fix the problem: "What should we do so this won't happen again?" Finally, find out what his goal is. If he wants to make something good to eat, suggest Construction Snacks as an alternative. If he just wants to pound his fists, then Oobleck may satisfy his need.

When kids have calmed down and have regained self-control, usually they will be agreeable to trying something different.

■ Helping Kids Get ''Unstuck'' ■

Some kids, though, will avoid new activities and will stick to one or two favorites. Up to a point, repetitions are fine, because children learn something new each time they practice a familiar action. However, a child who insists on doing the same thing in the same way may need help to get "unstuck." A possible solution to this situation is to show your own interest in a novel activity, and your child may cheerfully join in.

Once you get your kid started, back off and go about your own business. After all, the fun activities are meant to result in your child's very own work. *Some* attention, in the form of guidance, can spark a child's creativity: *too much* attention, in the form of control, can put a damper on it.

■ Talking Positively about Kids' Creations ■

Indeed, providing just the right kind of attention can be challenging. The trick is to speak positively. Talking positively is not always easy, but it is always important, whether you are commenting about your kid's art project or any other creative effort.

Here are some guidelines:

- Say, "Tell me about your work." This simple comment invites the child to express herself verbally as well as artistically. The child may say, "It's red," or "I used up all the toothpicks," or "Here's the whale, here's the fish, and here's the boat." Respond to what the child has said, with observations such as, "Yes, I see that you used only red food coloring for your Paper Towel Tie-Dye," or "You made a big pile of toothpicks!" or "I can see that the whale is spouting."

• If the child can think of nothing to say, you might encourage her with open-ended comments or questions that do not have a "yes" or "no" answer. For instance: "I see that this corner of the paper towel has turned orange. How do you think that happened?"

• Don't worry if your kid's Aiken Drum Face or Wood Scrap Sculpture is unrealistic. Young children, especially, are primarily interested in learning how to use the materials; their interest in representational art is secondary. Avoid questions that require the child to label or define ambiguous squiggles and shapes. Sometimes a hole is just a hole and a square is just a square.

• Suppose the child says, "This Lunch Bag Puppet looks terrible. I hate it." Acknowledge her feelings: "I guess you're disappointed after working so long." If she persists, saying, "It's ugly, isn't it?" you can answer, "I wouldn't say that it's ugly, but I do think that six eyes make it look very unusual." While you will want to make her feel better about her efforts, try to be honest. Honesty helps your kid develop the ability to criticize her own work.

• When the product is clumsy, messy, or not to your satisfaction, remember whose product it is. Your kid may be pleased with it. Although you may itch to straighten a line or add a flourish, remember that the process is the main purpose. You can say, "You really worked hard on that face!" or "You have a lot of original ideas," or "Each time you squirt glue, you get neater and neater."

• If the creation is gorgeous, phrase your praise carefully, saying, "That is really beautiful," rather than "You are such a good boy!" In other words, comment on the quality of the work, not on the quality of the child. Remember that the kid is not "a good boy" just because he is a good artist, anymore than he is "a bad boy" because his work is a mess.

• When the kid says, "Finished!" then he is finished. To prolong the activity, you can say, "Wow! You did that so fast! Want to make another one?" Avoid saying, "Finished already? But you just began! How do you expect me to get any of my work done?"

• If the kid says, "Clean up *now*? But I'm not finished," you can respond by saying, "I'm glad you're enjoying making that Mobile, but it's suppertime, and even artists have to eat. Let's move the pieces carefully to the corner so we can get dinner on the table. After we eat, you can work on it some more."

■ Ten Guiding Principles ■

Over the years, I have developed a "Tight Space Philosophy," with ten guiding principles:

1. Help your kids learn to be content in tight spaces.
2. Be prepared.
3. Be there.
4. Show your kids that you need them.
5. Provide multisensory activities.
6. Let your child choose the activity.
7. Give kids time.
8. When a kid must move, make moving possible.
9. Be tolerant of a little mess.
10. Take pleasure in your kids' pleasure.

The "Tight Space Philosophy" is explained on the next few pages. Please take a moment to read it—before the fun begins!

A TIGHT SPACE PHILOSOPHY

1. HELP YOUR KIDS LEARN TO BE CONTENT IN TIGHT SPACES.

Children are born with the urge to touch, move, take risks, make mistakes, and learn to become good problem solvers. They need a lot of space to satisfy this human urge.

Because tight spaces are unnatural, children naturally resist them. To learn how to be content in tight spaces, kids need guidance. You can help by offering fun activities to occupy their minds, soothe their anxieties, arouse their imaginations, and release their energies.

2. BE PREPARED.

Tight-space times are inevitable. Be ready!

When you are out and about, load your pockets or glove compartment with fun-activity equipment, such as a notepad, pencil, and piece of string.

Whenever you shop at the supermarket, hardware store, or toy store, pick up items that will come in handy when you most need them and least want to go out to buy them.

At home, you and your child can prepare areas specifically reserved for tight-space equipment. Stock a low kitchen shelf with supplies like flour, toothpicks, and plastic cups. Organize a drawer for paper, markers, pipe cleaners, buttons, etc. Fill a carton with dress-ups. Keep everything easy to get at and easy to put away.

3. BE THERE.

Even when you can't actually be with your children, assure them that you are there in spirit. If you are there to get them started with a Special Collection, for instance, your initial help will be the foundation of their growing interest. The collection will always remind them of your presence, even when you are elsewhere.

Later, if you spend a moment examining their collection when they ask, and occasionally contribute a button or bottle cap, your attention will show that you care. After kids learn how to proceed with a tight-space activity, your total attention will be unnecessary, because you will have given them the tools to play independently.

4. SHOW YOUR KIDS THAT YOU NEED THEM.

Kids in tight spaces can be world-class pests. Rather than hearing you say, "Stop bugging me and go find something to do," they will appreciate a suggestion for a specific activity that is useful and meaningful. Try saying, "I know you're at loose ends. Why not bring your crayons into the kitchen and make place cards for our dinner party tonight?"

Children always need to be needed, especially when they are stuck in a tight space—be it a small house, a sickbed, or a car seat. Many of the activities in this book, like Grocery Search or Ripping and Rolling Newspaper, teach kids valuable skills that are not only constructive and productive but are also good fun.

5. PROVIDE MULTISENSORY ACTIVITIES.

Different kinds of multisensory experiences help kids integrate their senses so that they feel competent and secure. Because movement, hands-on experiences, and learning all go together, it is logical that the more kids actively do, the more they can do.

6. LET YOUR CHILD CHOOSE THE ACTIVITY.

By all means, let your kid decide what to do. Considering the options and making a choice is half the fun. Choosing an activity gives kids a sense of control at the very moment when they feel they are being controlled by the tight space. Choosing also teaches kids how to make logical decisions, helps them develop problem-solving skills, and gives them an opportunity to pursue an interest of which you may be unaware.

7. GIVE KIDS TIME.

• *Give kids time to decide which activity to do.* Taking the time to deliberate before acting is a mature skill, and it is one to sponsor.

• *Give kids time to respond.* When you are playing a thinking game, like Fill-in-the-Rhyme, expect children to take longer than you would to respond. Let them speak for themselves, at their own pace.

• *Give kids time to finish.* Whether it is a thought, an art project, or a sifter full of flour, let kids have the satisfaction of completing the activity. (If you must tear them away for the schoolbus, dinner, or bedtime, give them at least five minutes' notice.)

• *Give kids time to wonder.* Sometimes they will seek tight spaces just to get away from it all. A child sitting quietly under a dining room table Secret Hideaway is busy thinking. Everybody needs a little time for reflection, so let the kid be!

8. WHEN A KID MUST MOVE, MAKE MOVING POSSIBLE.

(Actually, when does a kid *not* need to move?) When your kid is itching to escape from her airplane seat, you can give her movement sensations such as Joint Squeeze. The best thing you can do for a squirming kid is to show her how she can still move her muscles in tight spaces; the worst thing is to force her to be motionless.

9. BE TOLERANT OF A LITTLE MESS.

Some activities are messy, because creativity is messy. If you are a neatnik, try to relax. A little mud or disorder never hurt a child. Excessive neatness, however, hurts children very much by depriving them of hands-on exploration of their environment.

A kid absorbed in a Kite String Spiderweb or Smash Hit Cookies is not the neatest kid on the block. On the other hand, a kid absorbed in watching a video is very tidy, indeed. Which one will grow up to be resourceful and creative?

10. TAKE PLEASURE IN YOUR KIDS' PLEASURE.

Raising kids in tight spaces may be constricting, but a tight space does not imply a tight heart! Be free and wide with your approval, interest, and shared sense of fun while you have your kids in your brief embrace.

WHY THIS BOOK IS DIFFERENT

This book is not just another activity book. Sure, the ideas here, like ideas in other books, are educational and entertaining. Sure, some simple materials may be necessary. Sure, a parent, teacher, or caregiver usually needs to be on hand to get the activities going. So what makes *101 Activities for Kids in Tight Spaces* special?

1. All the suggestions included here have been specifically chosen to work in tight quarters, either indoors or in a confined spot such as a seat in a grocery cart or automobile.

2. The ideas are portable. What works in your home will also work in Grandma's house and in the classroom.

3. Anyone who can read can use these ideas. No special education in child development, science, art, music, physical education, occupational therapy, or French cooking is necessary! Many times I have heard parents say, "If only I had your training, I could come up with good ideas, too." Not so. All you need is what you already have: a child in a tight space.

4. Almost all the ideas are open-ended. (Exceptions are Road Sign Alphabet, which ends with *Z,* Fifty States License Plates Game, which ends when license plates from all fifty states have been found, and Kranberry Shapes, which ends when all the cranberry sauce has been used up.) The book's ideas are purposely intended to give your child control over how much time he or she wants to spend on each activity. The activities are over when the kid says so.

5. The activities are flexible, for flexible ideas make children wonder, and it is a sense of wonder that makes children active learners. In many cases your child will undoubtedly think up original ways to extend and revise the activities. For instance, your child may decide that a Windowsill Garden is so interesting that it may be fun to sprout onions, and maybe that will work. If it doesn't work, consider it a mistake for learning, for anytime a child does something, something is learned.

6. The activities do not require fancy equipment. Most of them assume that your home is equipped with basics such as pillows and blankets, water and shaving cream, string and paper. Look at these basics in a new light—they're the source of hours of tight-space activity!

7. The activities are appropriate for one child alone or for a child plus an adult or friend. No need to stage an elaborate birthday party or Labor Day picnic!

The book's purpose is to give you 101 successful, time-tested, kid-approved, on-the-spot, no-stress, fun, tight-space activities.

AGE RANGE

The activities are appropriate for boys and girls between the ages of three and ten. At the beginning of each activity, you will find a suggested age range.

In general, preschoolers, with their relatively short attention spans and emerging perceptual-motor skills, will get the most out of an activity when an adult or older sibling is nearby to help.

In general, elementary-school-age children, with their longer attention spans and maturing perceptual-motor skills, will be able to read the instructions independently and to carry out many of the activities without much adult intervention.

THE SETUP OF THE ACTIVITIES

This book is divided into five chapters. Each chapter suggests activities that are appropriate for a different kind of tight-space situation.

However, many activities work in more than one tight space. For instance, a child who is sick in bed may enjoy not only the ideas in chapter 3 but also many of those in chapter 1. Feel free to mix and match!

The activities are set up to include:

- A brief introduction
- A suggested Age Range
- What You Will Need—a list of necessary equipment or ingredients
- What to Do—step-by-step guidelines. Children who can read will be able to follow the instructions. Children too young to read will understand the instructions when an adult reads them aloud.
- Variations—ways to extend the ideas, where appropriate
- Helpful Hints for Grown-ups
- Learning Value—where appropriate

"THERE'S NOTHING TO DO"

(H O U S E B O U N D   A F T E R N O O N S)

■

S O M E   K I D S have lots of ideas for entertaining themselves—but many of these ideas are neither practical nor possible in a tight space on a nothing-to-do sort of day.

Other kids are too inexperienced or tentative to come up with amusing indoor activities on their own.

Both kinds of children will be sure to find something to engage their attention when choosing from one of the six types of activities in this chapter:

- Art and Carpentry Activities
- Nature and Science Activities
- Music and Sound Experiments
- Fun Food Activities
- Hands-on Activities
- Dramatic Play

Now, turn the page, and start having fun!

ART AND CARPENTRY ACTIVITIES

These are simple art projects, using simple equipment, that achieve satisfying products. Not only the product but also the process of creating an original work of art will delight your child. The activities are ideal for a tight space, such as a kitchen table or floor.

At the same time, kids develop important skills, such as:

• Using artists' tools to produce a Collage, a Mobile, a Newspaper Hat, Neat Place Cards, and three Punched Paper Activities (Chomp the Monster, Faces and Laces, and Paper Plate Tambourine)
• Using carpenters' tools for a Wooden Paddle Boat, a Nail Board, and If I Had a Hammer projects
• Creative thinking, as they imagine how a Lunch Bag Puppet, Soap Sculpture, or Wood Scrap Sculpture will look
• Fine-motor skills and eye-hand coordination, as they manipulate materials with their hands and fingers, such as folding paper towels for Paper Towel Tie-dye

■ Punched Paper Activities ■

Is your child feeling so cooped up that he wants to punch something? Here are a few activities made for the moment!

CHOMP THE MONSTER

Age Range: 3 to 7, with some help

What You Will Need
Hole puncher
Typing paper or construction paper
Pencil, crayon, or marker

What to Do
1. Draw a ghost or monster on the paper.
2. Punch holes in the picture until you have chomped up the ghost or monster.

FACES AND LACES

Age Range: 3 to 7, with some help

What You Will Need
    Hole puncher
    Shirt cardboard
    Cereal bowl
    Scissors
    Crayons or markers
    Yarn
    Large needle

What to Do
1. Place the cereal bowl upside down on the cardboard and trace around the rim to make circles.
2. Cut the circles out.
3. Draw faces on the circles.
4. Punch holes to make the eyes and the mouths.
5. Punch holes, about 1" apart, around the outlines of the faces and around the edges of the circles.
6. Thread the yarn through the needle and make a big knot.
7. Lace the yarn through the holes.
8. Tie additional lengths of yarn on to serve as hair.

PAPER PLATE TAMBOURINE

Age Range: 4 to 8, with some help

What You Will Need
    Hole puncher
    2 paper plates
    Crayons or markers
    Masking tape
    Yarn, threaded on a large needle
    Small jingle bells, or a few dried beans

What to Do

1. Decorate or draw pictures on the bottoms of the 2 plates.

2. Place the paper plates against each other, with their rims touching and bottoms facing out.

3. To keep the plates together while you work, tape the rims in two places.

4. Punch holes, about 1" apart, all the way around the rims of both plates.

5. Remove the tape.

6. Sew the plates together by lacing the yarn through the holes.

7. Stop lacing when you have about 6 holes left, to leave an opening.

8. Put the jingle bells and/or beans through the opening.

9. Finish lacing the plates together.

10. Shake, shake, shake your tambourine!

Helpful Hints for Grown-ups

• To minimize the cleanup of Punched Paper Activities, have your child work over newspaper to keep the punched-out circles in one place.

• When he is done, wrap the punched-out circles up carefully in the newspaper and throw them away, or save them to use another time for an art project like a Collage.

Learning Value

Using a hole puncher strengthens a child's:

• fine-motor skills in his fingers and hands,
• eye-hand coordination, and
• use of classroom tools.

■   ■   ■

■ Collage ■

A collage is a creative art project that any kid can do on the kitchen table or floor. Gathering the things to glue down is as much fun as arranging them into a beautiful design.

Age Range: 3 and up

What You Will Need
Piece of sturdy cardboard or a flat piece of wood for a base
Newspaper to protect the table or floor
White glue
Scraps of wood, toothpicks, craft sticks
Seeds and seedpods, pinecones, twigs, pebbles, shells, nuts, dried grasses and flowers, beans
Straws, cotton balls, corks
Fabric scraps, buttons, ribbons
Strips of newspaper or construction paper
Macaroni
Sequins and beads

What to Do
1. Put the cardboard, glue, and collage pieces on the newspaper.
2. Squeeze a blob of glue onto the cardboard base.
3. Stick a collage piece into the glue.
4. Add glue and different pieces until the collage looks finished.

Helpful Hint for Grown-ups
Making a collage is an open-ended project. Some kids love this activity and will take the time to cover every inch of the board. Others don't care for it and call it quits after gluing on the first cork. Everybody's different!

Learning Value

Collage making teaches kids how to express themselves artistically. Let your child decide how to arrange the pieces. If the arrangement pleases the child, then it is the process not the product that really matters.

■ Wood Scrap Sculpture ■

Making something out of nothing is fun on a "nothing" sort of day.

Age Range: 4 and up

What You Will Need

Wood scraps of different shapes and sizes
Sandpaper
White glue
Markers or paint

What to Do

1. Choose a wide, solid piece of wood to be the base for your sculpture. Sand it around the edges to remove the rough spots.

2. Choose smaller pieces of wood and sand them, too.

3. Onto the base, glue wood scraps together to make figures such as:

animals
people
houses and buildings
cars, trains, boats, and airplanes
fantastic designs

4. Press the pieces together for a moment after gluing in order to help them stick together. Use a *lot* of glue, because wood drinks it right up. The glue will be invisible when it dries.

5. Let the sculptures dry overnight.

6. After the glue is dry, decorate the Wood Scrap Sculpture with markers or paint.

Helpful Hint for Grown-ups

If you don't have wood scraps at home, go to a commercial lumberyard and tell the folks there that you would like scraps for children's art projects. The wood scraps are free for the asking, and you can usually take away as many as you can carry.

Learning Value

Making a Wood Scrap Sculpture:

- develops bilateral coordination (use of both hands together) and eye-hand coordination, and
- develops visual memory when a kid designs a sculpture to resemble a person or object he pictures in his mind's eye.

■ Paper Towel Tie-Dye ■

This art project requires a minimum of equipment and provides a maximum of pleasure.

Age Range: 3 and up

What You Will Need

Roll of absorbent paper towels
4 bowls of water
Food coloring
Newspaper (to dry the wet towels on)

What to Do

1. Dye the water with food coloring:
One drop will make a pale color.
Several drops will make a strong color.
Drops from 2 bottles will make a new color (mixing

red and blue makes purple, and mixing red and yellow makes orange).

Drops from 3 or 4 bottles will make a muddy brown color.

2. Fold a paper towel into tight squares or triangles.

3. Dip a corner of the triangle or square into a bowl of colored water. Dip a different corner into another bowl.

4. Open the paper towel, and look! The colors seep through the folds of the towel to make a gorgeous, bright, symmetrical design!

5. Spread the towels on newspaper to dry.

Variations

• Use coffee filters instead of paper towels.
• Use an eyedropper to drip the colored water onto the towels.

Helpful Hints for Grown-ups

• Smocks for younger children are a good idea, because food coloring stains.
• After the towels have dried, use them as place mats, doilies, wrapping paper, or an art display on the refrigerator.
• You can also frame the best one and send it to Grandma. She'll keep it forever.

■ Neat Place Cards ■

When company is coming, this idea is "neat" in three ways: (1) it makes guests feel welcome, (2) it makes the dinner table look pretty, and (3) it is quiet and tidy!

My niece, Katie Stern, thought up this fun activity herself. Like Kranberry Shapes, it has become one of our family's favorite Thanksgiving traditions.

Age Range: 6 and up

What You Will Need
3" × 5" file cards (white or colored)
Markers or crayons

What to Do
1. Make a list of the people who will be sitting down at the table for dinner. Remember to include your own family members.
2. Bring the short ends of the file cards together, and fold the cards in half. The unlined side should show. Now the cards can stand up like little tents.
3. Write a person's name on one half of each folded card.
4. Decorate each card around the person's name. Here are some suggestions:
   Holiday themes—pumpkins, snowflakes, Santa Claus, stars, wrapped gifts, flags, flowers, Easter eggs, firecrackers, etc.
   Symbols of people's jobs or hobbies—computer screens, telephones, books, apples, doctors' kits, paintbrushes, cars, trains, etc.
   Pretty designs from your own imagination
5. After the table is set, place a card above each plate so everyone will know where to sit. (A grown-up may need to help you put them in the right spots.)

Helpful Hint for Grown-ups
Children younger than six can do this, too. They may need help writing the guests' names.

■ **Fingerpainting with Shaving Cream** ■

No fingerpaints in the house? Try shaving cream. This activity feels good, smells good, and is easy to clean up, all at the same time. Furthermore, it takes only a little bit of space.

Age Range: 3 to 6

What You Will Need
Cafeteria tray or cookie sheet
Shaving cream

What to Do
1. Squirt a mound of shaving cream in the center of the tray.
2. With your sleeves rolled up, make designs in the shaving cream.
3. Write numbers, letters, or your name.
4. Make circles, squares, and triangles.

Variation
You could also fingerpaint with chocolate pudding or slightly coagulated jello. These are "finger-lickin' good" experiences!

Helpful Hint for Grown-ups
A painting smock is a good idea for a young child. If you don't have a painting smock, roll up the sleeves of an adult's shirt and let your kid use that instead.

Learning Value
Fingerpainting with Shaving Cream:

- provides a pleasantly messy tactile experience;
- gives kids the chance to practice making numbers, letters, and shapes; and
- lets kids "erase" their mistakes and start all over.

■ Lunch Bag Puppet ■

You don't need a great deal of space, great paints, or even great artistic talent to make a great puppet!

Age Range: 3 and up

What You Will Need
   Paper lunch bag
   Construction paper
   Scissors
   Glue
   Markers
   Scraps of fabric and yarn

What to Do
   1. Place the lunchbag in front of you, upside down. The bottom of the bag will be on top, ready to become the puppet's head.

2. Cut eyes, ears, a mouth, and a nose out of the construction paper.

3. Make eyebrows and hair out of yarn.

4. Decorate the bag to look like a person, animal, or monster.

5. "Dress" the puppet in fabric scraps.

6. Stick your hand up into the bag and put your fingers into the fold.

7. Move your fingers up and down inside the fold to make the puppet talk.

Learning Value

Making a Lunch Bag Puppet helps kids:

- observe where parts of the face are in relation to one another, especially if the kids are very young and/or do not seem to have a good sense of body awareness, and
- express emotions by designing an angry, sad, or happy face.

■ Mobile ■

Here is an art project that satisfies many needs of a kid with cabin fever. Deciding what objects to hang challenges the child's sense of creativity and aesthetics. Preparing the mobile fills empty time. Watching the finished mobile swing from the ceiling prolongs the pleasure.

Age Range: 5 and up

What You Will Need

Wire clothes hanger
Adhesive tape
Colorful yarn
5 lightweight objects to hang, such as:
    shells with holes in them
    pipe cleaners bent into interesting shapes or figures
    paper ornaments, such as origami figures
    buttons and beads
    little dolls and toys

What to Do

1. Bend the hook of the hanger into a loop. The end should touch the neck of the hanger. (A grown-up may need to help you.)

2. Wrap tape around the sharp end of the loop and the neck of the hanger.

3. Cut 5 pieces of yarn, about 12" long.

4. Tie one end of yarn to each object.

5. Attach the objects by tying the free ends of the yarn to the bottom of the hanger.

6. Hold the mobile in front of you and move the objects until they balance. The bottom of the hanger should be straight.

7. Tie a 3' length of yarn to the loop on top and tie the other end to an overhead light fixture or to an arch over a doorway.

8. Usually the mobile will rock gently in air currents made by a breeze coming through a window, the heat from the oven or radiator, or your movements in the room. If you want to make the mobile move more, try blowing at it through a drinking straw.

Learning Value

Making a Mobile encourages:

- fine-motor skills,
- a sense of balance, and
- eye-hand coordination.

■ Newspaper Hat ■

Here's an art project that is so simple, fun, and gorgeous that it will knock your socks off!

Age Range: 4 and up, with some help

What You Will Need
  Newspaper
  Masking tape and adhesive tape
  Feathers, ribbons, seam binding, lace and fabric
    swatches, buttons, yarn, paper flowers, fake fruit,
    small stuffed animals, etc.
  Mirror

What to Do
  1. Sit in front of the mirror. Center a couple of sheets of
  newspaper on your head. Pushing down on the newspaper, smooth it around your head, like an upside-down
  bowl, to make the crown of the hat.
  2. Wind masking tape around the crown in order to keep

the hat shaped just right. (Someone may have to help you.)

3. While the hat is on your head, use both hands, to make the brim of the hat by rolling the edges of the newspaper up toward the crown. Roll the brim all around the hat. If you squeeze the paper it will stay in place, nice and tight, but you can tape the brim in several places just to be sure.

4. Take the hat off and begin to decorate it. Use your best creativity! You can tape ribbons and feathers to hang from the brim, or stick a bunch of make-believe grapes to the brim, or perch a stuffed bird on the top. You'll look wonderful!

Helpful Hint for Grown-ups

Making a Newspaper Hat is one of those open-ended, stretchable activities that kids particularly enjoy doing with friends when they have a long afternoon to share together.

Learning Value

Constructing and designing a Newspaper Hat:

- provides kids with another accessory for the dress-up box, and
- gives them the opportunity to express themselves artistically.

■ Soap Sculpture ■

This is a good activity for whittling away the time. Not only is it interesting and creative, but it is also a multisensory experience. A child exercises the senses of touch, vision, and smell while manipulating the soap.

Age Range: 6 and up, with help

What You Will Need

Bar of soap
Toothpick or nail
Knife

What to Do

1. With the toothpick, draw the outline of a car, boat, animal, or whatever on the soap.
2. Carve around the outline, using the knife. Be careful!
3. Smooth the edges with wet fingers.

Helpful Hints for Grown-ups

• The tool used for this activity may be a plastic knife, a sharp paring knife, or a jackknife, depending on how careful and skillful the child is. The sharper the knife, the more precise the sculpture will be.
• You will probably need to supervise this activity.

■ Wooden Paddle Boat ■

You don't need a basement workbench or a lot of fancy tools to do this simple carpentry project, but you do need a bathtub.

Age Range: 4 and up, with some help

What You Will Need

Block of wood, about 4" wide, 6" long, and 1" thick. Pine is a good kind of wood for this project.
A small, thin piece of wood, about 1" wide and 2" long. A wooden ice cream spoon may work.
Sandpaper
2 nails, at least 2" long
Thick rubber band
Hammer

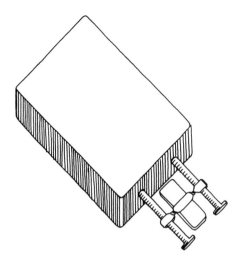

What to Do

1. Smooth the edges of the wood block with sandpaper. The wood block will be the "boat."

2. Stand the wood block on one of its narrow ends.

3. Hammer the 2 nails partway into the other narrow end. The nails should:

> stick out about 1½"
> be about 2" apart
> be about 1" in from the edge
> not wiggle

4. Put the rubber band around the 2 nails. Double the rubber band if it is very loose.

5. Before continuing, fill the bathtub with nice warm water.

6. Then, stick the little piece of wood into the space made by the rubber band. The little piece of wood is the "paddle."

7. Twist the paddle into the rubber band, in the direction away from the boat. Keep twisting. The rubber band will begin to get tight. Don't let go of the paddle.

8. Put the boat into the bathtub. Let go—and as the paddle untwists, the boat will zoom across the water.

9. Experiment with twisting the paddle. Twist it really tight and the boat will go faster and farther. Twist it *toward* the boat and see what happens. (The boat will go backwards.)

■ Nail Board ■

A Nail Board is an easy carpentry activity for an elementary-school-age kid to do right on the kitchen floor. When a kid feels cooped up, angry, or frustrated, hammering nails feels great.

Children of any age will enjoy arranging rubber bands on the nails into interesting shapes and patterns.

Age Range: 6 and up to make it
3 and up to play with it

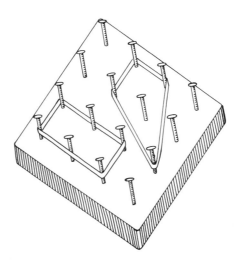

What You Will Need
Wooden board, about 12" square and about ½"–1" thick
Sandpaper
Hammer
Nails
Assorted rubber bands
Optional: tweezers

What to Do
1. Sand the wood until the edges are smooth.
2. Hammer nails partway into the board, about 1" apart, and not too near the edges. Any pattern is fine, but rows of nails are probably best. Don't hammer the nails all the way in. They need to stick up.
3. Test each nail to make sure it doesn't wiggle.
4. Stretch rubber bands over the nails to make a pretty design. Use your fingers or a pair of tweezers to move the rubber bands from nail to nail.
5. Play Nail Board games with another person:
Copy My Design: With rubber bands, one player makes a design of different shapes, like squares, triangles, and rectangles, on one half of the Nail Board. The next player copies the design on the other half of the board.
The Triangle Game: One player makes a triangle with a rubber band. The next player makes a triangle that does not overlap any other triangle. The person who makes the last possible triangle wins the game.

Helpful Hints for Grown-ups
• Some preschoolers will have the skills and patience to make a Nail Board with an adult's help. Children of elementary school age can make one alone, although it is important for you to be nearby in order to check over the work.

- If necessary, rub sandpaper over the block to get rid of any rough edges. Making a Nail Board is no fun if a kid gets a splinter.
- Check to make sure the nails are firmly in the board.
- If your child loads all the rubber bands between two nails, ignoring the rest, leave the design alone. A Nail Board is an open-ended toy—and anything goes!

Learning Value

Making and playing with a Nail Board increases:

- spatial perception,
- eye-hand coordination,
- basic understanding of geometric concepts, and
- game-playing skills.

■ If I Had a Hammer ■

Little kids like to hammer, too! Because their small hands aren't able to manipulate a real hammer, this wooden hammer activity will satisfy their wish.

Age Range: 3 and up

What You Will Need

To hit: large nails or golf tees
To hit with: wooden hammer or crab mallet
To hit into: foam blocks, such as packaging from new appliance cartons
Newspaper or carpet to protect the floor

What to Do

1. Put the foam blocks on the newspaper.
2. Hold the nails or golf tees in one hand and hit them into the foam blocks with the hammer.

Helpful Hints for Grown-ups
- No nails or golf tees? Put an egg carton upside down and let the child smash the cups until they are flat. Alternatively, provide a sheet of bubble wrap to smash.
- No wooden hammer? Give the child a real hammer, a bunch of nails, and a split fireplace log. (A split log will lie flat on the floor.) With your supervision, let her drive the nails into the log.

NATURE AND SCIENCE ACTIVITIES

Children are naturally curious about the world they inhabit. Especially if your family lives in tight quarters in an urban community, your kids' opportunities for actively exploring an outdoor environment may be limited.

These activities sponsor:

- Observations of creatures such as insects and birds, when kids make a homemade Bug Jar or a Pinecone Bird Feeder
- Experimentation with water, one of Mother Nature's greatest gifts, when they play with Waterdrop Doggies
- Skills in growing and caring for living plants, when they experiment with the six projects in a Windowsill Garden (Avocado Plant, Vegetable Greens, Potato Plants, Corn-on-the-Sponge, Mystery Plant, and Terrarium)

■ Bug Jar ■

Bugs are interesting to collect, study, and then let go. A fancy bug jar isn't necessary, because a homemade bug jar is simple to make and works as well.

Age Range: 3 to 7, with help
8 to 10, without help

What You Will Need

Small cake tin, or a tin that nuts came in
Piece of aluminum screen or wire mesh (available from
a hardware store) about 8" × 24"
String or dental floss

What to Do

1. Make a cylinder by overlapping the narrow ends of the aluminum screen.

2. Set the screen cylinder into the cake tin.

3. Trim the screen if necessary.

4. With string or dental floss, tie the overlapping edges of the screen together in a few places.

5. Set the cake tin lid on top of the cylinder. Presto! You have your very own Bug Jar!

6. Collect caterpillars, lightning bugs, grasshoppers, or other insects that are too big to escape through the holes in the screen.

7. Gather some leaves from the place where you found the insects and put the leaves into the jar, too.

8. After watching the bugs for a while, let them go. No living thing likes being in a tight space for too long!

Helpful Hints for Grown-ups

• If you are squeamish and uncomfortable handling insects, it is still a wonderful idea to give your child an opportunity to pick them up gently with bare hands and place them in the Bug Jar.

• If your kid is the one who is uncomfortable handling insects, you can collect the bugs and put them into the Bug Jar. Then your child will still have the chance to observe them. A child who is reluctant to handle wriggling bugs still may be extremely interested in looking at them.

Learning Value

Making and filling a Bug Jar gives kids lessons in:

- using their hands to manipulate objects,
- collecting insect and plant specimens,
- observing nature, and
- caring for the environment.

■ Pinecone Bird Feeders ■

In the wintertime, birds have to work hard to find enough to eat. Making a few Pinecone Bird Feeders will help them.

Age Range: 3 and up

What You Will Need

Several big pinecones
Peanut butter
Small bag of birdseed
2 pie pans or plates
String or yarn

What to Do

1. Put a big blob of peanut butter in one pie pan and a mound of birdseed in the other.

2. Roll the pinecones around in the peanut butter first and in the birdseed next.

3. With your fingers, pat the birdseed all around the pinecone so that it sticks well to the peanut butter.

4. Tie a length of string to each pinecone.

5. Hang the pinecones on a tree branch outside a window. Before long, hungry birds will discover this unexpected winter treat.

6. Count the number of birds you see nibbling at the feeder.

7. Make a list of the kinds of birds you see, or get somebody to help you write the list. You can find books about birds at the public library.

Helpful Hint for Grown-ups

Some children are allergic to peanut butter. Even touching or inhaling it may cause an allergic reaction. If that is the case with your child, use solid shortening instead.

Learning Value

Making a Pinecone Bird Feeder encourages:

* fine-motor skills,
* knowledge and interest in urban wildlife, and
* understanding of the term "pecking order."

■ Waterdrop Doggies ■

Playing with a drop of water is an activity that is simply amazing and amazingly simple, all in a very tight space.

Age Range: 3 and up (younger children will need adult supervision)

What You Will Need

Optional: eyedropper
Glass pie pan or glass casserole dish
Toothpick
Paper printed with words or pictures
Drop of dish detergent
Paper towel

What to Do

1. With your finger (or an eyedropper), put a single drop of water in the glass pie pan. This is the "Waterdrop Doggie."
2. Look closely at the Doggie. Notice its domelike shape.
3. Push the Doggie around the pan with your finger.
4. Push the Doggie with the toothpick.
5. Prick the Doggie with the toothpick to separate it into smaller drops, or "Puppies."

6. Push the Puppies together again to form one big Doggie.

7. Hold a paper printed with words or pictures under the pan, and look at the paper through the Doggie. The print will look bigger, because the waterdrop is like a magnifying glass.

8. Squirt a little dish detergent on the Doggie. Whoosh! The Doggie will collapse.

9. Touch the paper towel to the runaway Doggie. Goodbye, Doggie!

Variations

• Put a spoonful of water into 4 small cups. Add a drop of red food coloring to the first cup, green to the second, yellow to the third, and blue to the fourth. Waterdrops from these bowls will look like beautiful jewels. Push red and yellow drops together to make orange, and red and blue together to make purple.

• Find a picture of a Christmas tree or a lady's face. Slide the picture under the glass pan. Decorate the glass-covered picture with colored waterdrops that look like ornaments or jewelry.

• Instead of a glass pie pan or glass casserole dish, use a piece of wax paper—but be careful not to let the Doggie run off the edge.

Helpful Hint for Grown-ups

Waterdrop Doggies is an easy yet exciting activity for children of all ages. The antics of the Doggie and Puppies are so interesting that your kid will surely want to discuss them with you. Seize the moment to share this meaningful science lesson!

Learning Value

Experimenting with Waterdrop Doggies encourages curiosity about scientific principles such as:

• surface tension (the physical force that constricts the surface of the waterdrop into the shape of a dome),

• adhesion (the tendency of the waterdrop to stick to a glass-top table, a finger, a toothpick, or a piece of wax paper),

• cohesion (the tendency of several waterdrops to stick together),

• magnification (the ability of water to act like a lens to increase the apparent size of words or pictures seen through it),

• emulsification (the ability of detergent to break down the surface tension of the waterdrop), and

• absorption (the ability of the paper towel to soak up the waterdrop).

■ Windowsill Garden ■

Sure, anybody can grow parsley on a windowsill, if you go to a gardening center and buy the right kit. But it is a hundred times more meaningful to grow plants from fruits and vegetables that a kid finds in the kitchen.

AVOCADO PLANT

Age Range: 3 to 5, with help
6 to 10, without much help

What You Will Need
Avocado pit
4 toothpicks
Jar of water
Soilless potting mix (available from a hardware store or gardening center)

What to Do
1. Hold the avocado pit with the pointed end up and stick the toothpicks into the seed about 1" below the tip.

2. Place the pit into the jar, filled with enough water to cover about half of the pit. The toothpicks will rest on the lip of the jar and will keep the pit from falling.
3. Add water when the water level gets low.
4. In a few weeks, roots and leaves will appear. Transplant the plant into a pot of soilless potting mix.

Variation

You can also start an avocado plant by planting the seed directly in soilless potting mix. To do this:

- Fill a 4" flowerpot halfway with potting mix.
- Put the seed, pointed tip up, in the pot.
- Add more potting mix so that about ¾" of the seed sticks out above.
- Water the mix until it feels damp to the touch.
- Put the pot on the windowsill and keep it watered.

VEGETABLE GREENS

Age Range: 3 to 5, with help
6 to 10, without much help

What You Will Need

Vegetables (edible roots), such as:
beets
carrots
onions
radishes
Knife
Pie pan or roasting pan
Roasting rack or cookie rack that will fit into the pan
Water

What to Do

1. Put the rack into the pan.
2. Slice the carrots, turnips, and radishes about ½" from the top.

3. Place the vegetable tops on the rack.

4. Put enough water into the pan to cover the bottoms of the vegetable tops.

5. Put the pan next to a sunny window. In a few days, shoots will begin to grow.

6. Remember to add fresh water to the pan whenever the water level gets low.

Variation

If you don't have a roasting rack or cookie rack that fits into the pan, you can also use an aluminum screen. Here is what to do:

• Cut out a piece of screen that is a little larger than the bottom of the pan you're using.

• Bend under the edges of the screen and set it into the pan. You will want the screen to be slightly raised off the bottom of the pan so that roots have space to grow under it.

Helpful Hint for Grown-ups

Kids can plant the vegetable tops after they have rooted, but it is unlikely that anything edible will grow indoors or survive for very long.

POTATO PLANTS

Age Range: 3 to 5, with help
6 to 10, without much help

What You Will Need
White potatoes
Toothpicks
Plastic cups
Water

What to Do

1. Cut out chunks of white potato surrounding the "eyes." The eyes are buds that will grow into new plants.
2. Stick 3 toothpicks around each chunk, near the top.
3. Rest the toothpicks on the rims of the cups.
4. Fill the cups with water. The bottom halves of the chunks should be covered by the water. The eyes are above the water.
5. Put the cups on a sunny windowsill.
6. Add water whenever necessary.

Variations

• You can also put the potato chunks on a rack or piece of screen that is resting on the bottom of a pan.
• Grow a sweet potato plant. Leave the sweet potato whole. Stick toothpicks into it. Find the end that has no purple buds on it and set this end into a cup of water. Pretty soon, a lovely vine will begin to grow.

CORN-ON-THE-SPONGE

Age Range: 3 to 5, with help
6 to 10, without help

What You Will Need

Corn on the cob or popcorn kernels
Pie pan
Clean sponge
Water

What to Do

1. Put the sponge into the pie pan.
2. Put enough water into the pan to soak the sponge.
3. Lay the corn on top of the sponge.
4. Put the pan next to a sunny window. In a few days, green shoots will begin to grow.
5. Add water when the sponge gets dry.

MYSTERY PLANT

Age Range: 3 to 5, with help
6 to 10, without help

What You Will Need
Seeds from fruits such as oranges, grapefruit, lemons,
tangerines, apples, watermelons, etc.
Plastic cups or flowerpots
Commercial soilless potting mix (available at hardware
and garden stores)

What to Do
1. Fill a couple of cups with soilless potting mix.
2. Place 2 or 3 different seeds into the cup.
3. Water the seeds. Wait a few days and watch what
happens.

TERRARIUM
A terrarium is a miniature garden that grows within a covered plastic or glass container. In an enclosed environment,
the plants use and reuse the same water in a cycle that involves evaporation and condensation.
Talk about living in a tight space! Your kid will really dig
making a terrarium.

Age Range: 4 and up, with some help

What You Will Need
A container, such as:
glass jar
fishbowl
plastic shoe box
Plants, such as:
rooted cuttings of ivy, begonia, coleus, or spider plant
mosses from outdoors

little flowering plants
ferns
tree seedlings
acorns
Gravel or sand
Soil or potting mix
Water
Plastic wrap

What to Do

1. Clean the container.
2. Cover the bottom of the container with ½" of gravel or sand. This will provide proper drainage.
3. Fill the bottom third of the container with soil or potting mix.
4. Moisten the soil just enough so that little bits stick together in balls when you press it with your hand.
5. Stick your fingers into the damp soil to make holes for the plants.
6. Put the plants into the holes.
7. Water the plants.
8. Cover the container with plastic wrap.
9. Put the terrarium near a window that does not get direct sunlight. Too much sunlight will scorch the plants.

Variations

• Make a terrarium container out of a large, clear plastic soda bottle. Cut off the top of the bottle, leaving a base about 8" tall. After preparing the soil and plants inside, insert an upside-down plastic drinking cup firmly into the top to keep in the moisture.
• Add small pieces of bark, little rocks, and tiny ceramic forest creatures to make the terrarium look like a miniature landscape.
• At a garden center, buy some mimosa seeds. Mimosa seeds germinate easily and look like miniature trees.

Helpful Hint for Grown-ups

If the water level inside the terrarium is perfectly balanced, you will notice water droplets forming on the sides and top of the terrarium. If no water droplets form, then the terrarium needs more water. If the sides are always very wet, then the terrarium has too much water. Remove the plastic wrap for a few hours in order to let some excess water evaporate.

Learning Value

Growing plants in a Windowsill Garden teaches kid to observe:

- development of roots, stems, and leaves,
- vegetative propagation (growing new plants from seeds of old plants),
- photosynthesis (the process involving sunshine, air, and water that plants with green chlorophyll use to grow),
- phototropism (the movement of plants toward sunlight),
- differences in the physical properties of seeds, vegetable tops, and tubers (potatoes), and
- the water cycle of evaporation and condensation.

MUSIC AND SOUND EXPERIMENTS

Every child is a born musician. Given the chance, kids will develop their innate interest in rhythm and pitch and become equipped with the tools to enjoy making music, throughout their lives. These activities will:

- Provide opportunities for kids to respond emotionally and creatively to the mood and tempo of instrumental recordings, when they are Drawing to Music
- Produce quick and easy "musical instruments" suitable for a homemade rhythm band, such as a Rubber-Band Harp, a Chicken Squawker, and a Jingle-on-a-Stick

- Connect classic children's literature with purposeful activity at the piano, during Keyboard Stories
- Teach kids how to make real music, with a Waterglass Xylophone

■ Drawing to Music ■

This activity is perfect for a day when kids are feeling closed in. It's an open-ended art project that gives cooped-up muscles a workout while some great instrumental music plays in the background. (Most of the music listed below is classical, simply because that is what I know best. Jazz and pop music work just as well!)

Age Range: 3 and up

What You Will Need
  Newspaper or plain newsprint paper
  Crayons (not markers)
  Recorded instrumental music, such as:
      Anderson's *Syncopated Clock*
      Bach's Air on a G String and *Arioso*
      Beethoven's Symphony no. 6 (*Pastoral*)
      Bizet's *Children's Games* and *L'Arlésienne* Suite
      Bolling's Suite for Flute and Jazz Piano
      Brahms's Variations on a Theme by Haydn
      Chopin's Piano Concerto no. 1
      Debussy's *Golliwog's Cake Walk*
      Dukas's *The Sorcerer's Apprentice*
      Dvořák's *Humoresque* and *Slavonic Dances*
      Elgar's *Pomp and Circumstance Marches*
      Grieg's *Peer Gynt* Suite
      Grofé's "On the Trail" from *Grand Canyon* Suite
      Handel's *Water Music* and *Music for the Royal Fireworks*
      Haydn's "Toy" Symphony
      Mendelssohn's *A Midsummer Night's Dream*

Mozart's Piano Concerto no. 21 and Variations on a Nursery Rhyme ("Twinkle, Twinkle")
Pachelbel's Canon in D
Prokofiev's *The Love for Three Oranges*
Ravel's *Mother Goose* Suite
Rossini's *William Tell* Overture
Saint-Saëns's *Carnival of the Animals*
Schubert's String Quintet in A Major (*The Trout*)
Schumann's *Carnaval* and *Scenes from Childhood*
Smetana's *The Moldau*
Tchaikovsky's *The Nutcracker* Suite and *1812 Overture*
Vivaldi's *The Four Seasons*
Villa-Lobos's *The Family of Dolls.*

What to Do

1. Play some instrumental (not vocal) music. Classical music or jazz works well.

2. Place newspaper and a bucket of crayons (not markers) on the floor.

3. Lie (not sit) on the floor and draw whatever and however the music inspires you.

Variation

Drawing to Music is an activity you can also enjoy sitting up, in the car, in bed, or even in the doctor's waiting room. All you need is paper, crayons, and music coming from a radio or headset.

Helpful Hints for Grown-ups

• Instrumental music is better than vocal for this activity, because the point is to let the rhythm and melody of the music, rather than the lyrics, inspire the child's movements.

• Crayons are best for two reasons: (1) kids need to use their fine-motor muscles in their hands and fingers to bear down firmly in order to produce color, and (2) kids can produce dark or light colors to match the music. Markers don't have these advantages.

• Lying on their stomachs to draw requires kids to stretch their heads up and their arms and legs out—and it is stretching, not slumping, that they need to do in tight spaces.

• If your child doesn't seem to know how to get started, here are some things to talk about:

Tempo. Is the music fast or slow? Can you make your crayon move as quickly or as slowly as the music?

Dynamics. Is the music loud or quiet? Can you make your crayon accompany the music with big, exuberant swoops or with small, soft squiggles?

Mood. Is the music sad, joyful, questioning, jumpy, jolly, gentle, angry, etc.? Can you make your crayon draw designs that match the music, such as graceful spirals or jagged mountains?

Color. Does the sound of the music make you think of a certain color? Can you find a crayon to match?

Rhythm. Do you feel or hear the patterns of the musical beats? Can you make your crayon draw along with the rhythmic patterns?

Learning Value

Drawing to Music teaches kids:

• to appreciate fine music;

• to become conscious of different qualities of music and sound (auditory discrimination);

• to develop beat awareness, an important skill for moving, speaking, and even reading smoothly; and

• to develop muscular control in their torsos, legs, arms, hands, and fingers.

■   ■   ■

■ Rubber-Band Harp ■

This used to be called a cigar-box harp, but people seem to smoke fewer cigars these days, so cigar boxes are harder to find. That's okay because you don't need a cigar box, anyway, to make this interesting musical instrument.

Age Range: 4 and up

What You Will Need
> Cigar box or sturdy cardboard box, about the size of a shoe box but stronger than a shoe box
> Assortment of rubber bands

What to Do

1. Pick up a few rubber bands, one at a time, and find out which are stretchy and which are not very stretchy. Big, skinny rubber bands are usually the best ones to use for this activity.

2. Choose a stretchy rubber band and pull it over the narrow end of the box.

3. Bring the rubber band toward the middle of the box.

4. Plunk the rubber band with your finger. When the rubber band vibrates, it makes a sound. Can you hear it?

5. Add as many more rubber bands as you wish.

6. Adjust the rubber bands so that there is a little space between them. They shouldn't touch. If they touch, they won't have room to wiggle back and forth (vibrate). They must vibrate in order to make sounds.

7. Strum your Rubber-Band Harp by moving your fingers back and forth across all the rubber bands at once.

8. Pluck your Rubber-Band Harp by pulling one rubber band at a time.

9. Sing a song or march in place as you strum or pluck.

Variations
- Adjust the rubber bands to make higher or lower sounds:

  Pulling on the rubberbands is a temporary tuning technique. Eventually the tension will equalize around the box.

  Make a *higher* sound by pulling the rubber band *down* on both sides to make it tighter across the top of the box and looser across the bottom.

  Make a *lower* sound by pulling the rubber band *up,* so it is looser across the top of the box.
- Make another Rubber-Band Harp on a box that is a different size. The bigger the box, the bigger the sound.

Helpful Hints for Grown-ups

- Making and playing a Rubber-Band Harp is an ideal project for a tight space because it is a very quiet activity. Rubber bands don't make much noise!
- If all the rubber bands are the same size, don't worry. Your kid can still have fun adjusting them to learn about the qualities of sound.

Learning Value
Making and playing a Rubber-Band Harp:

- develops tactile discrimination, when kids handle rubber bands that are fat and skinny, little and big, and stretchy and not very stretchy;
- teaches awareness that stretching different sizes of rubber bands requires different amounts of muscular force;
- teaches awareness that the size and tension of an object affect its vibrations (skinny, tight rubber bands make more vibrations than fat, loose rubber bands); and
- teaches awareness of the differences in musical pitch, or frequency (skinny, tight rubber bands make higher sounds than fat, loose rubber bands).

■ Chicken Squawker ■

The advantage of this activity is that it is unbelievably simple, quick, and amusing. It is especially fun when several kids make and play their Chicken Squawkers together.

The disadvantage is that Chicken Squawkers are noisy, so it is best to do this activity when a big ruckus in a tight space won't bother anybody.

Age Range: 6 and up

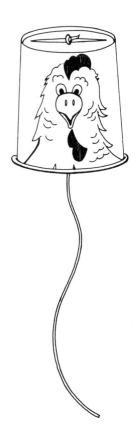

What You Will Need
Plastic drinking cup (the kind you can draw on)
Toothpick
2' length of string
Markers

What to Do
1. Using a toothpick, poke a hole in the center of the cup's bottom.
2. Knot one end of the string to the middle of the toothpick.
3. Using the toothpick, push the free end of the string through the hole, into the cup.
4. Grasp the string with your fingers by reaching inside the cup.
5. Pull the string through the hole until the knot makes it stop.
6. Decorate the cup with the markers. Draw the head of a chicken or a picture of a barn.
7. Now the fun begins! Hold the cup upside down in your left hand (if you are right-handed). Using the tips of your right thumb and index finger, pull down on the string in short jerks. Do you hear a squawk? Practice until you do.
8. Play your Chicken Squawker while singing "Old Mac-Donald Had a Farm." It's even more fun—and a lot funnier—when you sing along with a few friends!
9. Crowd into the bathroom and play your Chicken Squawkers for an even better effect.

■ Jingle-on-a-Stick ■

This rhythm instrument is fun to make and fun to play.

Age Range: 4 to 6, with help
7 to 10, without much help

What You Will Need

2 bottle caps
Plank of thick wood
Hammer
Large nail or awl
Small common nail
Washer
About 6" length of thick wooden dowel or old broomstick

What to Do

1. Place the bottle caps, ridges down, on the plank of wood. With the big nail (or awl) in one hand and the hammer in the other, punch a hole into the center of each cap. (Ask a grown-up to help.)

2. Smash the caps flat with the hammer.

3. Make a "jingle sandwich" by placing the washer between the 2 caps.

4. Prop the dowel on its end.

5. Hammer the small nail through the jingle sandwich and partway into the top of the dowel. Make sure that the nail is tight enough not to wiggle, but not so tight that the caps and washer can't jingle.

6. Shake your Jingle-on-a-Stick while singing—what else?—"Jingle Bells"!

Helpful Hint for Grown-ups

The process of making a Jingle-on-a-Stick is noisy, because it involves hammering. However, the sound it makes when a kid plays it is very quiet.

Learning Value

This activity provides more than fun:

• Punching holes in the bottle caps and making a "jingle sandwich" develop fine-motor skills and eye-hand coordination.

• Pounding the caps flat strengthens the upper body and

provides kids with an outlet for their tight-space aggression.

• Using hammers, awls, and nails teaches kids how to handle carpentry tools.

• Shaking the Jingle-on-a-Stick improves a sense of rhythm.

■ Keyboard Stories ■

Even preschoolers who are too young to read music will have fun retelling familiar stories this novel way.

Age Range: 3 to 6, with help

What You Will Need
Piano or electronic keyboard

What the Grown-up Is to Do
1. Stand side by side at the piano.
2. The adult says, "Let's tell the story of 'Goldilocks and the Three Bears' at the piano."
3. Show the child four areas on the keyboard where the four story characters "speak." Strike a few bass notes at the far left of the keyboard. Say in a low, deep voice, "This is how the Papa Bear sounds when he talks."
4. Play a few notes an octave or two higher, but below middle C. Say in a regular, adult voice, "This is how the Mama Bear sounds."
5. Play a few notes above middle C. Say in a girlish voice, "This is how Goldilocks sounds."
6. Play a few treble notes at the far right of the keyboard. Say in a squeaky, babyish voice, "And this is how the Baby Bear sounds."
7. Say, "Do you want to be the Papa, the Mama, the Baby, or Goldilocks?" If your child wants to be more than one character, that's fine, of course.
8. Begin telling the story. Whenever it is time for a char-

acter to speak, accompany the spoken words with a few notes in the appropriate range.

Variations for Grown-ups and Kids to Share

• Extend this musical activity by playing other familiar stories with four or five distinct characters:

"The Three Billy Goats Gruff" (three Billy Goats and a mean Troll)

"The Three Little Pigs" (three Pigs and a big, bad Wolf)

"Little Red Riding Hood" (Little Red Riding Hood, Mother, Grandmother, Woodsman, and Wolf)

"The Gingerbread Man" (Gingerbread Man, Old Lady, various farm animals, and the Fox)

"The Bremen Town Musicians" (Donkey, Dog, Cat, Rooster, and Robbers)

• Simplify this activity for very young children, or for children who have a short attention span, by telling stories that have only two or three "voices":

Caps for Sale by Esphyr Slobodkina (Peddler in the bass range and a group of Monkeys together in the treble range)

"Little Miss Muffet" (Little Miss Muffet and the Spider)

The Runaway Bunny, by Margaret Wise Brown (Mother Rabbit and Little Bunny)

Swimmy, by Leo Lionni (the Big Tuna, Swimmy, and the school of fish)

• Make up your own stories!

Family stories (Grandpa, Daddy, Mommy, siblings, etc.)

Classroom stories (teacher, classmates)

Animal stories (squirrels, dogs, cats, etc.)

Helpful Hints for Grown-ups

Telling Keyboard Stories provides an opportunity for a parent and child to snuggle up close. They take only a few minutes, and on a day when space is tight and tempers are short, a shared activity with a common goal may be just what the doctor ordered.

Furthermore, musical talent is not required!

Learning Value
Telling Keyboard Stories:

- teaches kids how to use a piano or keyboard purposefully,
- introduces the musical concept of pitch to suggest the voices and personalities of different characters,
- reinforces classic children's literature, and
- gives kids the chance to express their thoughts and emotions through sociodramatic play.

■ Waterglass Xylophone ■

Here is an excellent activity to entertain your child in a corner of the kitchen. A Waterglass Xylophone is a set of eight drinking glasses filled with water to produce the eight notes of a musical scale.

You are probably familiar with a xylophone. A xylophone is a musical instrument with eight wooden bars. (*Xylo* and *phone* come from the Greek words for "wood" and "sound.") From left to right, the xylophone's wooden bars get gradually smaller in size and higher in sound, or pitch. Together, the eight bars make a musical scale. (*Scale* comes from the Latin

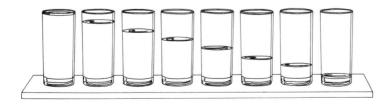

word for *ladder,* and a ladder is just what a xylophone looks like.)

A Waterglass Xylophone works on the same scientific principles as a xylophone. Instead of wooden bars, however, this homemade instrument uses water to produce musical pitches.

Preparing and playing this musical instrument is extremely intriguing.

Age Range: 5 and up, preferably with an adult nearby

What You Will Need

8 identical water glasses (20 ounces, if possible)
Pitcher
Dishpan filled with water
Wooden mallet or spoon
3 bath towels
8 adhesive labels, marked 1, 2, 3, 4, 5, 6, 7, 8

What to Do

1. Spread 2 bath towels on the kitchen floor. Place the waterglasses in a row on one towel. Set the dishpan onto another towel. Save the third bath towel to wipe up spills.

2. Dip the pitcher into the dishpan and fill it with water. Pour water into the first glass, all the way to the brim. Strike the glass with the mallet. The sound you hear will be the first, lowest pitch of your musical scale, or octave—Pitch #1.

3. Pour water into the second glass, but a little less than went into the first glass. Slightly less water in the glass produces a slightly higher sound. A slightly higher sound is what you want to make the second glass Pitch #2.

4. Strike #1 and #2. If you think #2 is too high, add more water. If you think #2 is too low, pour out some water into the dishpan.

5. If the two sounds please you, continue filling the other six glasses to produce Pitches #3, #4, #5, #6, #7, and #8. By the time you get to the last glass, you will need just a few drops of water, or no water at all.
6. Strike #1 and #8. They should have the same musical pitch, an octave apart.
7. Adjust the water levels in the 8 glasses until you are satisfied with your Waterglass Xylophone.
8. Stick the adhesive labels on the glasses, numbering them from 1 to 8.
9. Now you can play real tunes! Following are the beginnings of some familiar melodies.

PLAYING REAL TUNES
To play real tunes, read the numbers from left to right, just like reading words across a page. Strike the mallet on the waterglass that matches the number you read. When you see a dash (-), that means you should rest, and not hit a waterglass.

"JOY TO THE WORLD"	8	7	6	5
	Joy	to	the	world,
	4	3	2	1
	The	Lord	has	come.
"FRÈRE JACQUES"	1	2	3	1
	Frè-	re	Jac-	ques,
	1	2	3	1
	Frè-	re	Jac-	ques,
	2	3	4	—
	Dor-	mez	vous?	
	2	3	4	—
	Dor-	mez	vous?	

"MARY HAD A LITTLE LAMB"	3 Ma-	2 ry	1 had	2 a
	3 Lit-	3 tle	3 lamb,	—
	2 Lit-	2 tle	2 lamb,	—
	3 Lit-	5 tle	5 lamb.	—
"THIS OLD MAN"	5 This	3 old	5 man,	—
	5 He	3 played	5 one,	—
	6 He	5 played	4 nick-	3 nack
	2 On	3 my	4 thumb.	—
"LONDON BRIDGE"	5 Lon-	6 don	5 Bridge	4 is
	3 Fall-	4 ing	5 down,	—
	2 Fall-	3 ing	4 down,	—
	3 Fall-	4 ing	5 down.	—
"TWINKLE, TWINKLE"	1 Twink-	1 le,	5 twink-	5 le,
	6 Lit-	6 tle	5 star,	—
	4 How	4 I	3 won-	3 der
	2 What	2 you	1 are.	—

"OLD MACDONALD"	4	4	4	1
	Old	Mac-	don-	ald
	2	2	1	—
	Had	a	farm,	
	6	6	5	5
	Ee-	i,	ee-	i,
	4	—	—	1
	Oh,			and
	4	4	4	1
	On	this	farm,	he
	2	2	1	—
	Had	a	cow,	
	6	6	5	5
	Ee-	i,	ee-	i,
	4	—	—	—
	Oh.			

BEETHOVEN'S NINTH	3	3	4	5	5	4	3	2
SYMPHONY	1	1	2	3	3	2	2	—
	3	3	4	5	5	4	3	2
	1	1	2	3	2	1	1	—

Helpful Hint for Grown-ups

Do not expect a kindergartner to produce a perfectly pitched scale by pouring water into the glasses. Even an elementary-school-age kid may need your help. While precise measuring will produce satisfying musical pitches, precision is not as important as the process of making a Waterglass Xylophone. Don't worry if the pitches don't sound exactly right to your ears. Your kid will have fun, and that is the main point of this tight space activity.

Variations

• Stick numbers on a real xylophone or on the piano's middle C scale and try these tunes.

• Put different amounts of water into 8 plastic soda bottles, and blow into them.

Learning Value
Preparing and playing a Waterglass Xylophone is a multisensory activity that strengthens:

• eye-ear-hand coordination,
• left-to-right reading skills,
• the ability to distinguish between sounds (auditory discrimination),
• the ability to remember and reproduce tunes that the child has heard (auditory memory and sequencing), and
• the joy of making music!

FUN FOOD ACTIVITIES

Preparing food may be a chore for grown-ups, but it is a pleasure for kids, especially when they come up with something edible. These activities, requiring simple ingredients and very little counter space, help kids:

• Understand math concepts, such as counting raisins for Ants on a Log or sunflower seeds for Footprints in the Snow
• Combine ingredients to produce appealing and nutritious snacks or meals, such as Aiken Drum Faces, Construction Snacks or Muffin Pizzas
• Feel a sense of accomplishment when the kitchen experiments turn out to taste surprisingly good, as in Baked Surprise
• Prepare pretty Kranberry Shapes for a holiday meal

■ ■ ■

■ Ants on a Log ■

Ants on a Log is a nutritious and delicious recipe that will appeal to your child's sense of the ridiculous. Preparing this recipe also proves that working in the kitchen is fun.

Age Range: 3 and up

What You Will Need

Vegetable brush
Knife (a serrated butter knife, rather than a sharp paring knife, is good for a preschooler to use)
Celery
Peanut butter
Raisins

What to Do

1. At the kitchen sink, use the vegetable brush to scrub the celery ribs clean.
2. Cut the ribs into 2 or 3 sections.
3. Spread peanut butter on a celery section and line up a few raisins on top. It doesn't matter how much peanut butter or how many raisins go on the celery "log."
4. Arrange them on a plate and serve them to your family.

Learning Value

For young children, this activity helps develop math concepts. Here are some questions to ask:

• How many "ants" are on each "log"?
• If you add two more ants to a log, how many will there be?
• If you subtract three, how many will be left?
• Which log has the most ants? Which has the fewest?

■ Footprints in the Snow ■

Footprints in the Snow is a variation of Ants on a Log.

Age Range: 3 and up

What You Will Need
  Celery ribs, prepared as for Ants on a Log (page 61)
  Cream cheese
  Sunflower seeds

What to Do
  1. Fill the celery ribs with cream cheese.
  2. Count out 4 sunflower seeds.
  3. Place the seeds close together on the cream cheese so that they look like a tiny animal's pawprint.
  4. Count out 4 more seeds and make another pawprint, and another, and another, until you come to the end of the celery rib.

■ Aiken Drum Faces ■

Aiken Drum is the name of a whimsical, musical, edible character celebrated in a Scottish folk song.

"AIKEN DRUM" SONG

There was a man, lived in the moon,
Lived in the moon, lived in the moon,
There was a man, lived in the moon,
And his name was Aiken Drum.

And he played upon a ladle, a ladle,
A ladle,
And he played upon a ladle,
And his name was Aiken Drum.

And his face was made of cream cheese . . .

And his eyes were made of raisins . . .
And his mouth was made of an apple slice . . .
And his hair was made of carrot shreds . . .

Age Range: 3 and up

What You Will Need
Round rice cakes
Cream cheese
Raisins for eyes
Apple slice for the mouth
Carrot shreds for hair
Butter knife for spreading
2 spoons to beat together while you sing

What to Do
1. Spread the cream cheese on the rice cake.
2. Add Aiken Drum's eyes, mouth, and hair.
3. Sing or chant Aiken Drum's song while beating time on the spoons. In the song, Aiken Drum uses big soup ladles to keep a musical beat, but you may have more fun playing the spoons, which are like miniature ladles.
4. Eat your delicious, nutritious Aiken Drum Face!

Variations
• Like other open-ended folk songs, "Aiken Drum" begs for variations and additions. What other kitchen instruments might Aiken Drum have played upon? What other foods might his facial features have been made of? Make up your own verses to sing or chant, such as:
And he played upon the pie pans . . .
And he strummed across the cookie rack . . .
And he beat upon the soup pots . . .
And his face was made of peanut butter . . .
And his eyes were made of blueberries . . .
And his nose was made of sunflower seeds . . .
• Use a toasted English muffin instead of a rice cake as a base for his crazy face.

Learning Value

- Making up new verses teaches about the concept of "theme and variations."
- Keeping time, by striking a pair of spoons together, reinforces beat awareness.
- Designing an Aiken Drum Face helps a young child become aware of body parts.

■ Construction Snacks ■

Playing with food is thoughtless when so many people in the world don't have enough food to eat. However, Construction Snacks fall into a different category, because you can eat the product.

Age Range: 3 and up

What You Will Need

Pretzel sticks
Cheese cubes

What to Do

1. Connect cheese cubes with pretzel sticks, the way you build with construction toys. See if you can make the frame of a building, or a robot, or a porcupine.

2. Eat your construction.

Learning Value

Constructing these snacks teaches kids about spatial relationships.

■ Muffin Pizzas ■

These are tasty treats.

Age Range: 4 and up, with minimum help

What You Will Need

English muffins

Tomato sauce

Mozzarella cheese, grated or sliced

Oregano

Optional: mushrooms, green pepper, bacon bits, sausage, pepperoni, anchovies, Parmesan cheese, thyme, or any other favorite pizza topping

Cookie sheet

What to Do

1. Split the muffins and toast them.

2. Spread 2 tablespoons of sauce on each muffin half.

3. Add any topping.

4. Top with cheese.

5. Sprinkle oregano on top of the cheese.

6. Place the muffins on the cookie sheet.

7. Ask for help to broil the Muffin Pizzas for a few minutes until the cheese melts.

■ Baked Surprise ■

Great cooks come up with new dishes by experimenting. Who knows what will happen when a kid concocts a Baked Surprise? It may be surprisingly delicious!

This is a great activity for the kid who wants to be creative in the kitchen without feeling limited by a specific recipe. In fact, precise measurements have been left out on purpose. The point of this cooking experience is not precision, but freedom to experiment.

Age Range: 4 and up

What You Will Need
Large mixing bowl
Long-handled spoon and a spatula
1 or 2 eggs
Flour
Milk
Cooking oil
Sugar
Baking soda
Square baking pan
Pat of margarine or butter on a paper towel, or
   no-calorie spray
Other ingredients, such as raisins, oatmeal, chopped ap-
   ples, chocolate chips, peanut butter, etc.
Toothpicks

What to Do
1. Turn on the oven and preheat to 350° (ask for help, if necessary).
2. Prepare the baking pan by rubbing the margarine or butter around the inside. Be sure to get the corners greased, too. Or use Pam or some other no-calorie spray instead.
3. Break the egg into the bowl and stir it well.
4. Add one or two cups of flour and a little milk. Stir well.
5. Add a spoonful of cooking oil, a spoonful of sugar, and a pinch of baking soda. Blend well.
6. Add one or more of the other ingredients.
7. When the mixture looks like cake dough, put it into the greased baking pan.
8. Put the pan into the oven and bake for 20 or 30 minutes, or until a toothpick comes out clean.
9. Taste your Baked Surprise, and if it's good, share it!

Helpful Hint for Grown-ups
A Baked Surprise is a worthwhile activity even if it doesn't turn out to be delicious. Think of it as an experiment in cook-

ing and science. Kids learn by doing—and by making mistakes as they go.

Learning Value

Making a Baked Surprise is a multisensory activity that teaches:

- measuring and blending (perceptual motor skills),
- a sense of mastery in the kitchen, and
- a sense of feeling useful and needed.

■ Kranberry Shapes ■

Especially at holidays, when grown-ups are busy with company and meal preparations, kids seem more underfoot and restless than usual. Here's an idea: Instead of kicking children out of the kitchen, invite them in and give them something useful to do.

Age Range: 4 to 7, with minimum help
7 and up, with no help

What You Will Need

Can of jellied cranberry sauce (1 can per child)
Cookie cutters
Knives
Serving plate
Bowl

What to Do

1. Open the can at one end and remove the lid. Throw the lid away carefully.

2. Place the can upside down on the serving plate.

3. Open the can at the other end. It is important to do this over the serving plate in order to catch the drips.

4. Gently push down on the lid to slide the cylinder of jellied cranberry sauce out of the can.

5. Lay the cylinder of cranberry sauce on its side.
6. Slice carefully through it to make about 10 circles.
7. Lay the circles down on the serving plate.
8. Press cookie cutters into the cranberry circles.
9. Remove the excess cranberry sauce and put it into a bowl for tomorrow's leftovers.
10. To go with the holiday roast, serve the prettiest cranberry sauce ever!

Helpful Hints for Grown-ups

• Preschoolers will probably produce funny-looking Kranberry Shapes. They may be paper thin, or exceedingly thick, or poorly trimmed. But who cares how they look, when your proud, helpful, beaming child brings the plate to the company table?

• Kids who get to make Kranberry Shapes remember the ritual all their lives. I am happy to share our family tradition with you!

HANDS-ON ACTIVITIES

This section includes activities that involve kids' active touching and manipulation of objects. The more that children get their hands on objects, the more they learn about the objects' physical properties, such as texture, shape, size, weight, and density. And the more children touch, the more they learn!

This catchall section includes a variety of activities that encourage:

• Concentration and attention, when kids build a House of Cards or a Domino Lineup
• Concepts of classification, sequencing, and organization, in Sorting Jobs, Special Collections, and Memory Box
• Tactile and spatial perception, when kids weave a Kite String Spiderweb or construct a Marble Chute
• Game-playing skills, in Marbleship Battle

■ House of Cards ■

This activity requires a steady hand, a long attention span, and a low frustration level.

Age Range: 7 and up

What You Will Need
Deck of cards
Sturdy table to work on

What to Do
1. Very carefully, stand 2 cards on their narrow ends, about 2" apart.
2. Supporting the 2 cards gently with one hand, take a 3rd card and lay it like a bridge across their tops.
3. Very, very carefully, right next to this construction, set up another construction with 3 more cards.
4. Very, very, very carefully, build out and up with more cards. This activity takes a lot of concentration and practice!
5. When the construction falls over, begin again. How many cards can you use?

Helpful Hints for Grown-ups
• Building a House of Cards is an engrossing tight-space activity for a child with a lot of patience and manual dexterity. It is probably not an activity to suggest to a kid who tends to be impulsive or who gets frustrated easily.
• This activity seems to work better on a table than on the floor. Having the cards closer to eye level makes the difference.
• Cards that have been well-used may be easier to build with than brand-new cards. The soft, worn edges of used cards are less slippery than the edges of new cards.

■ Domino Lineup ■

Lining up dominoes and watching them fall is wonderfully amusing on a rainy day.

Age Range: 3 and up

What You Will Need
> Set of dominoes
> Clear space on a table or floor

What to Do
> **1.** Stand a domino up on its narrow end.
> **2.** Line up the other dominoes close to, but not touching, one another. Make a long row, until you have used up all the dominoes.
> **3.** Touch the first domino. As it falls, it will make the next one, and the next one, and the next one tip over. This is what people mean when they talk about "a domino effect."

Variations
> • Make a curved row and watch them fall.
> • Build a Domino House—much easier to construct than a House of Cards!

■ Sorting Jobs ■

Sorting, or classifying, is an important skill, and it's fun, too.

Age Range: 3 to 5

What You Will Need
> Egg carton, fishing tackle box, bobbin box, or kitchen utensil tray
> Household or "found" objects such as buttons, coins,

beans, shells, pebbles, beads, costume jewelry, crayon stubs, poker chips, paper clips, etc.

What to Do
1. Sort by color, kind, shape, or size.
2. Dump everything out and do it again!

Variations
* Line up the objects to make a long, snaky road.
* Trade objects with a friend.
* Sort playing cards:
  Red and black piles
  Heart, diamond, spade, and club piles
  Number and picture piles
  In numerical order
* Help sort the laundry.

Learning Value
A child engaged in Sorting Jobs strengthens many developmental skills:

* visual discrimination, by seeing differences in the shape and size of objects,
* tactile discrimination, by feeling differences in textures, shape, and size of objects, and
* perceptual-motor coordination, by using hands and eyes together.

A child also strengthens many math concepts:

* classification, by grouping objects by color, kind, or shape;
* computation, by counting, adding, and subtracting objects;
* seriation, by arranging objects in order, according to size (from small to big), or according to intensity of color (from dark to light); and

• sequencing, by putting one object in the first compartment, two in the second, three in the third, etc.

■ Special Collections ■

Working on a collection may be very pleasing—and a child can give it as much or as little time as he wants.

Age Range: 3 and up

What You Will Need

Odds and ends that are lying around the house, such as:
bottle caps
spoons
pencils
seashells, rocks, and pebbles
flowerpetals
postage stamps (canceled and uncanceled)
autographs (start with the family)
sewing buttons
lapel buttons, such as I LIKE IKE or SAVE THE WHALES

A place to put the collectibles, such as:
shoe box
egg carton
fishing tackle box
bobbin box or sewing box with many compartments
box of see-through drawers (the kind carpenters use for hardware)
notebook (for autographs, stickers, or stamps)

What to Do

1. Gather the things.
2. Sort them.
3. Label them.
4. Put them in boxes or notebooks.

Helpful Hints for Grown-ups

• Help your kid get started by showing some interest—but not too much! It's fine to suggest what to collect or how to display the objects, but if your child has a preference, don't insist that your method is better. Remember whose collection this is.

• If your child already has a collection, remind him about it. (Kids who complain about being bored often forget how many interesting activities there are to do.) You might say, "Gee, I haven't seen your stamp notebook in a long time. This postcard that Uncle Pete sent from Mexico has a beautiful stamp. Want it?"

• Respect whatever your kid collects, even if collecting bottle caps seems silly to you.

Learning Value

A Special Collection:

• improves abilities to observe and classify,

• encourages a kid to read up on the objects he collects, and

• provides a frame of reference for socializing with other children who collect the same things.

■ Memory Box ■

A Memory Box has three major purposes:

1. On a tight-space afternoon, when a kid has nothing to do, loading the box with treasures she wants to save forever occupies her for some time.

2. It frees up precious shelf and floor space by getting the never-ending clutter together in one place.

3. It provides a source of great pleasure on another tight-space day when the kid opens the box and revisits the memories stored inside.

Age Range: 3 and up

What You Will Need

A cardboard sweater box (available in hardware and variety stores),

Adhesive stick-on letters and numbers

What to Do

1. On a rainy day, load the box with report cards, team photographs, first-grade papers, bulky works of art, and old collections of football cards or dinosaur stickers.

2. A few months later, on another rainy day, pull out the box and take a look.

3. When the box is full, stick letters on the lid to spell out your name and the years in which you produced the papers and art—for instance, "HAYLEY, 1994–1996."

4. Store the Memory Box in a safe, dry, out-of-the-way space and replace it with another and another.

Helpful Hints for Grown-ups

• Before getting a Memory Box, decide where you will store it. If you want to keep it under your child's bed, buy one that is shallow enough to fit (about 6" high). Bigger things will need a taller box and a space such as a closet floor or shelf. Wherever you put the Memory Box, be sure that your child can get at it easily.

• It isn't important that papers be placed in order. Some kids really like to sort and classify things by date or by subject, while others don't like doing that at all. The point of a Memory Box is to get all the keepsakes safe and together in one place.

• Even if your kid doesn't want to save anything, YOU could make a catchall Memory Box for items such as medical records, preschool artwork, and elementary school report cards. But . . . if you make a Memory Box, then it's YOUR fun activity, and not your child's!

• Never, ever get rid of a Memory Box without your child's permission.

■ Kite String Spiderweb ■

Kids like this activity more than grown-ups do. It's great!

Age Range: 7 and up

What You Will Need
Kite string

What to Do
1. Take the end of the string and tie it to a bedpost.
2. Let out the string and wrap it around a dresser drawer knob.
3. Now tie it to the closet door handle. Keep going until the room is a huge spiderweb.
4. Invite friends and family to crawl through the web.
5. Before going to bed, untie all the knots.

Variation
At Halloween time, you can get make-believe spider-webbing material at a toy store. It's fun to "web" the house, around doorways and window frames. And cleaning up is not hard at all.

Helpful Hints for Grown-ups
• Weaving a Kite String Spiderweb is wonderful fun, but untying it is a big bore. Your kid probably isn't going to want to clean it up, so you will need to decide whether he must take down the entire web, or just part of it, before bedtime. (Your major concern will be to make sure that there is a clear path from the bed to the door-way, in case he needs to get out of his bedroom in the

middle of the night.) Therefore, it is important to establish ground rules with your kid before he gets started.
* Don't try to save the string. It's hopeless.

Learning Value
Making and crawling through a Kite String Spiderweb:

* encourages fine-motor skills and eye-hand coordination,
* develops motor-planning skills, and
* provides a novel tactile experience.

■ Marbleship Battle ■

This is a competitive game of skill for two or more players.

Age Range: 7 and up

What You Will Need
For each player:
> 3 large marbles for Battleships,
> 6 medium-size marbles for Destroyers, and
> 10 small marbles for Fighters;
> or, if your marbles are all the same size, use different-colored marbles for each role.

Plastic container to keep marbles in
Smooth floor
Several bath towels

What to Do
1. Roll up a few bath towels into loose sausages and arrange them in a circle on the floor. The circle will be the battle site. The towels will keep the marbles from rolling all over the place.
2. Sit on a towel or on the floor inside the circle.
3. Each kid, as an Admiral of a fleet of marbles, chooses his or her marble "ships."

4. The object of this game is to wipe out the other Admiral's marble fleet. Players take turns aiming and shooting their marbles at the other Admiral's marbles. Hitting another Admiral's ship entitles the player to take an extra turn.

5. If you hit a small Fighter once, you will "sink" it, and the other Admiral has to take it out of the game.

6. If you hit a medium-size Destroyer twice, you will sink it.

7. If you hit a large Battleship three times, you will sink it. You have to remember!

8. You can use a Fighter, Destroyer, or Battleship to hit the other Admiral's Marbleships.

9. Make up your own rules!

Helpful Hint for Grown-ups

The rules to this game are very flexible. Kids will want to make up new rules as they go along, and that's just fine. You won't need to help them—and they won't want your help anyway.

Learning Value

Marbleship Battle develops:

- game-playing skills,
- social skills and communication skills, and
- attention span and memory.

■ Marble Chute ■

A Marble Chute made out of paper towel rolls is a very simple, very satisfying activity that works well in tight spaces. In fact, the tighter the space, the more interesting it becomes to create a pipeline for marbles to roll through.

Age Range: 4 to 6, with help
7 and up, without help

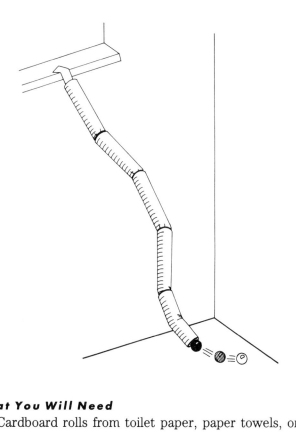

What You Will Need

Cardboard rolls from toilet paper, paper towels, or gift-wrap paper

Masking tape

Scissors

About 6 marbles

Plastic cup or bowl

What to Do

1. Sit on the floor. Hold a cardboard roll in one hand and drop a marble through it. Where did the marble land? In your lap? Under the couch? Now rest one end of the roll on the floor and the other end on one foot, and let go of a marble. How far does it roll?

2. Gently squeeze the end of the cardboard roll and fit it into the end of another cardboard roll. Maybe you will want to add a third cardboard roll to make a long, straight pipe.

3. Now you may want to add an elbow to the chute to make a curved path for the marbles. You can make an elbow by bending cardboard rolls a little bit. (If you bend them too much, the marbles won't be able to get through.)

4. Add cardboard rolls and elbows until you have a long chute. When you are pleased with the path, tape all the parts together.

5. Tape the high end of your marble chute to a window-sill or a chair.

6. Place a plastic cup or bowl at the low end to catch the marbles.

7. Have fun!

Variations

• Use cardboard mailing tubes (the kind posters come in) to make a chute for rubber balls.

• If you need elbows that are more flexible than cardboard, make tubes out of sheets of paper by rolling them lengthwise.

DRAMATIC PLAY

Play is the work of children. Whenever kids play the part of another character, they experiment with being in someone else's shoes. Make-believe strengthens all areas of a child's development:

• Cognitive development, by reinforcing the child's cultural heritage, restoring order and meaning to events the child has observed, and providing a sense of beginning, middle, and end

• Emotional development, by addressing universal emotions, rehearsing adult roles, and releasing tension or resolving conflict

• Social development, by expanding a child's make-believe repertoire, encouraging turn taking and flexibility, and actively engaging a child in a shared experience

• Motor development, by suggesting different ways to move and encouraging motor planning (the ability to think of and carry out a novel movement sequence)

• Language development, by strengthening listening and speaking skills, and reinforcing vocabulary that the child has heard in real-life situations

In this section, you will find instructions for:

• Nursery Rhyme Playlets: "Little Miss Muffet," "Jack Be Nimble," "Little Bo Peep," and "Little Jack Horner"

• Fairy Tale Playlets: "The Three Little Pigs" and "The Three Billy Goats Gruff"

• Real Life Playlets: "Shoe Store," "Barbershop," and "Classroom"

• Secret Hideaway

■ Nursery Rhyme Playlets ■

To act out nursery rhymes and fairy tales, you don't need a big stage—just a little floor space.

''LITTLE MISS MUFFET''

Age Range: 3 to 7, with help

What You Will Need
Cushion
Plastic bowl
Large spoon
5 black pipe cleaners
3' of yarn or stretchy thread
2 kids

What to Do

1. Make a "spider" puppet by holding a bunch of 4 pipe cleaners and bending them in half.

2. Twist the 5th pipe cleaner around the middle of the pipe cleaner bunch to make a "spider body."

3. Arrange the 8 spokes to make "spider legs."

4. Tie one end of the yarn or stretchy thread to the body.

5. Place the cushion, bowl, and spoon on the floor. The cushion is Little Miss Muffet's "tuffet" (a small grassy mound). The bowl and spoon are for her "curds and whey" (cottage cheese).

6. The kid playing Little Miss Muffet sits on the cushion and pretends to eat her snack.

7. The kid playing the Spider holds the puppet by the string and stands a few feet away.

8. Recite the "Little Miss Muffet" rhyme. When the Spider hears "Along came a spider," he walks up to Miss Muffet, dangling the puppet in his hand.

9. At the words "and sat down beside her," the Spider puts the puppet on the floor next to Miss Muffet.

10. Miss Muffet tosses the bowl and spoon away and leaps off the tuffet.

11. Miss Muffet and the Spider exchange places and enact the rhyme again.

Variation

No pipe cleaners? Put a plastic or rubber spider (the kind kids collect at Halloween) on a string.

Helpful Hints for Grown-ups

Some kids are born actors. They don't require any urging to engage in dramatic play. They will love dramatizing little playlets, with or without props, with or without costumes— even with or without you.

Other kids, however, do need a grown-up to "set the stage." If acting out little stories doesn't come naturally to them, they need help and practice to learn how to play dramatically.

Because make-believe is so important for helping a child develop in all ways, please join in your child's dramatic play in every tight-space situation.

Learning Value

Dramatizing "Little Miss Muffet," and the other nursery rhymes suggested on the next pages:

- develops language and communication skills,
- develops sociodramatic skills that help kids interact with others in positive and meaningful ways,
- allows kids to address universal emotions and to work out feelings through expressive play, and
- improves motor planning.

"JACK BE NIMBLE"

Age Range: 3 to 7, with help

What You Will Need

Candle stub (about 2" long)
Wad of aluminum foil

What to Do

1. Make a little candleholder out of the aluminum foil by squeezing it around the bottom of the candle so that the candle will rest in it and stand up straight.
2. Put the candle on the floor.
3. Stand near the candle.
4. Recite, "Jack be nimble, Jack be quick, Jack jump over the candlestick."

5. Jump over the candlestick when you say the word "*over.*"

"LITTLE BO-PEEP"

"Little Bo-Peep" is a one-minute drama that includes loss, suspense, separation anxiety, and joyous reunion. Most preschoolers will be delighted to exchange parts and to repeat this playlet many times. It is very meaningful to them, as you will see.

Age Range: 3 to 5, with help

What You Will Need
Xylophone and mallet
Stick or branch, about 2'–3' tall, with a "crook" to resemble a shepherdess's staff
Large potted plant, to hid the sheep
3 or more people

What to Do
1. Decide who will be the lost sheep, Little Bo-Peep (or Little Joe-Peep), and the "orchestra."
2. Set the scene:
> The lost sheep crouch silently behind the potted plant, pretending to be out of sight.
> Little Bo-Peep holds the staff and stands in front of the plant, pretending not to notice the sheep.
> The orchestra gets ready to play the "Little Bo-Peep Scale Song." To play the song, hit the xylophone bar that matches the number. Begin with 8, the smallest bar.

3. While the orchestra plays the song, everyone can sing along.
4. During the song, Little Bo-Peep walks around the room. She pretends to search for her sheep, but she *does not look back.*
5. Meanwhile, the sheep quietly crawl behind her.

6. As the song ends, Little Bo-Peep arrives back at the plant. Turning to see the sheep behind her, she says, "There you are!"

7. The sheep say, "Here we are!" and pretend to wag their tails.

8. Exchange roles and repeat, and repeat, and repeat.

"LITTLE BO-PEEP SCALE SONG"

8	7	6	5
Lit-tle Bo-	Peep has	lost her	sheep and

4	3	2	1
can't tell	where to	find	them.

1	2	3	4
Leave them a-	lone and	they'll come	home,

5	6	7	8
wag-ging their	tails be-	hind	them.

Helpful Hints for Grown-ups

• If the bars of your xylophone are not already numbered, write the numbers 1, 2, 3, 4, 5, 6, 7, and 8 on adhesive labels and press the labels on the bars. The biggest bar is 1; the smallest is 8.

• The song can also be played on a piano or a Waterglass Xylophone.

• Little Bo-Peep's song is a scaled-down "Pathétique." All the great symphonic *pathétiques,* such as Tchaikovsky's Symphony no. 6 in B minor, opus 74, employ descending scales to express great sadness, and ascending scales to express joy and hope.

At the beginning of her story, Little Bo-Peep is a pretty sad character, so a descending scale accompanies her anxious search for the sheep. Then, as she nears the place where she started, the scale ascends, and the story and song are resolved on a joyful note.

Learning Value
Playing the Little Bo-Peep story helps kids develop empathy. Appreciating Little Bo-Peep's predicament, they sense what it feels like to be given some responsibility—and then to "blow it." They are in her shoes.

When Little Bo-Peep and the sheep are reunited, kids are overjoyed. It is just amazing to observe!

''LITTLE JACK HORNER''

Age Range: 3 to 5, with help

What You Will Need
Pie pan
Several large stringing beads (one of which is purple or blue)
Tight space, like a corner of the room

What to Do
1. Decide who will be Little Jack Horner (or Little Jill Horner) and who will recite the nursery rhyme.
2. Little Jack Horner sits in the corner, with the pie pan and loose beads in his lap.
3. The person reciting says:

> "Little Jack Horner
> Sat in a corner
> Eating his Christmas pie.
> He stuck in his thumb . . ."

4. Little Jack Horner sticks his thumb into the purple bead.

5. The person reciting continues:

> *"And pulled out a plum,*
> *And said . . ."*

6. Little Jack Horner says,

> *"What a good boy am I!"*

■ Fairy Tale Playlets ■

Like Nursery Rhyme Playlets, Fairy Tale Playlets help a kid grow in all areas of development: cognitive, emotional, social, language, and motor.

Keyboard Stories (page 53) is another activity in this book that suggests fairy tales as a source of tight-space fun. In a slightly wider space than at the piano, you can also dramatize fairy tales.

Please note: The best stories for playlets are usually those in which children and animals are the primary characters. Technically, these stories are termed folk tales or nursery tales, rather than fairy tales, which require elves, fairies, dragons, or other magical creatures. However, *fairy tales* is a suitable catchall phrase for our purposes.

Here's how to produce a couple of old favorites:

''THE THREE LITTLE PIGS''

Age Range: 3 to 7, with help

What the Grown-up Will Need
Familiarity with the story
A few props that are essential to the story, such as straw, sticks, and a few bricks (or drinking straws, pencils, and kids' construction blocks)
Costumes (optional)
3 or 4 restless kids

What the Grown-up Is to Do

1. Introduce the story in one of two possible ways:

Tell it in true oral tradition. Without visual aids, kids develop their imaginations as they picture characters and scenes in their mind's eye. You may darken the room and even light a candle or beam a flashlight toward the ceiling to evoke a sense of wonder and mystery.

Read the story aloud. Feel free to add or subtract parts of the printed version. If your kid is a purist and complains that you are reading it wrong, explain that a fairy tale is told so many times by so many people that many versions exist, and that's okay.

2. Set the scene. You might want to use masking tape to mark spots on the rug or floor where the story characters are supposed to go.

3. Say, "Here is where the Littlest Pig builds his house. Here is where Middle Pig and Big Pig go. Over here is where the Wolf waits."

4. Ask the kids what parts they want to play.

If they all want the same part, say, "We can act this story out several times so that everybody gets to do what he wants. Let's take turns."

If a kid can't decide, suggest, "How about the Middle Pig? He gets to build with these nice sticks." Or suggest that the child pair up with another kid. It's okay to have two Middle Pigs once in a while.

Helpful Hints for Grown-ups

• Be flexible! Producing playlets is an inexact science. Children will forget their lines, speak out of turn, change their minds about being the Wolf after all, reinvent dialogue, rearrange props, and be charmingly unpredictable. Roll with the punches, and enjoy!

• Kids love grown-ups to get into the act, so take a part yourself now and then.

* Invite kids to be the narrator. Some will leap at the chance to be the storyteller.
* Build a birthday party around a Fairy Tale Playlet theme.
* Try other stories, too. The easiest ones to produce as playlets have a small cast of characters, simple dialogues, repeated phrases, and a brief storyline. Here are a few suggestions:
    Books:
    Are You My Mother? by Philip D. Eastman
    Caps for Sale, an east European story, by Esphyr Slobodkina
    It Could Always Be Worse, a Yiddish folk tale, by Margot Zemach
    Mr. Gumpy's Outing, by John Burningham
    Stories:
    "The Bremen Town Musicians"
    "The Gingerbread Man"
    "Goldilocks and the Three Bears"
    "Little Red Riding Hood"
    "Peter and the Wolf," a musical tale by Sergei Prokofiev
    "The Shoemaker and the Elves"
    "The Three Billy Goats Gruff" (the next activity)
* Some stories are difficult to reproduce as playlets because they are too long, have too many characters, present technical problems, or are completely unmanageable—the last thing you need in a tight space! To save you time and trouble, here is a list of stories that I have found to be less successful:
    "Cinderella"
    "Hansel and Gretel"
    "Rapunzel"
    "Seven Little Kids"
    "Snow White"
    Where the Wild Things Are, by Maurice Sendak
    The Wizard of Oz, by Frank Baum

''THE THREE BILLY GOATS GRUFF''

This is a classic Scandinavian tale that many American children have in their repertoire. If you are not familiar with it, you can find it at the library or in a bookstore.

Age Range: 3 to 7, with help

What the Grown-up Will Need

Familiarity with the story

Table that children may walk on (the "bridge")

2 chairs to help Billy Goats climb onto and off the table (place 1 chair at each end of the table with its back against the table)

4 cushions or mats (place 3 on the floor to the left of the table for the 3 Billy Goats to sit on while they wait for their turn, and place the 4th under the table for the Troll)

Potted plant on the floor, to the right of the table

4 kids

What the Grown-up Is to Do

1. Tell the story.

2. Show the kids:

Where the Billy Goats will sit, how they will cross the "bridge," and how they will gather around the plant after they make it safely across.

Where the Troll will sit (under the bridge).

3. Ask the kids what parts they want to play and help them get into their positions.

4. Begin to narrate the story: "Once upon a time . . ."

5. When the playlet is over, applaud, change casts, and repeat.

Helpful Hints for Grown-ups

• When you first tell the story, introduce the characters as females. If the boys in the group resist playing the part of a female goat, you can say, "It's okay for boys to pretend to be girl goats. Girls pretend to be boy goats all the time." Little girls appreciate this.

• Change the story to "The Three Dinosaurs Tough." Instead of billy goats, the protagonists could be plant eaters such as stegosaurus, brontosaurus, and triceratops. Instead of a troll, the antagonist could be a meat eater such as tyrannosaurus rex.

• In the classic version, the biggest Billy Goat butts the Troll on the head with his horns. Head butting requires good coordination on the part of the Billy Goat and trusting cooperation on the part of the Troll. Suggest tapping the Troll lightly on the head with the fingertips as a gentler and easier alternative.

• This playlet also works well with a cast of six children. Two Trolls can sit together under the bridge, and four Billy Goats can go trip-tropping across it. A larger cast than six, however, tends to become unmanageable.

■ Real Life Playlets ■

Got a few minutes? That's all it takes for you, together, to act out little stories about people who are familiar to your child. Enacting familiar scenarios gives your child a chance to "try out" adult roles and to develop important social skills.

Take turns being "the Kid" and "the Grown-up." It may be surprising to see how children behave when they imitate big people.

After you and your child have dramatized these neighborhood scenes once or twice, you can bow out and let your child and a friend continue the play.

SHOE STORE

Age Range: 3 to 6, with help

What You Will Need
2 or 3 pairs of shoes (shoes do not need to be new)
Shoehorn
Optional: shoe boxes, shoe polish, and new shoelaces

What to Do
1. Decide who will be the shoe shopper and who will be the shoe salesperson.
2. The shopper says, "I am looking for some brown shoes."
3. The salesperson says, "Here are some very nice shoes. Would you like to try them on?"
4. Go through the motions and conversation involved in trying on shoes, choosing just the right pair, and paying for them.
5. Extend the play by putting new laces into the holes of shoes or by polishing the shoes so they'll look as good as new.
6. Exchange roles.

Helpful Hints for Grown-ups
• Sociodramatic play (playing make-believe with another person) is most meaningful when kids assume the roles of people they know. Kids have observed how parents, teachers, storekeepers, and doctors speak, move, and respond in real-life situations. Thus, kids have some idea of appropriate language and behavior.
• Sociodramatic play is less meaningful when kids pretend to be superheroes or TV characters. Often, these characters have personalities that are either good or bad, powerful or weak. Their range of emotions and reactions is limited, and so when kids imitate them in sociodramatic play, their emotional range is equally limited.
• While a few simple props improve the play, props are not essential. Whenever or wherever your child is in a tight space, proposing a make-believe scene is always appropriate!

BARBERSHOP

Little girls will especially love this activity. Little boys love it, too. It feels good, and it's fun.

Age Range: 3 and up, with help

What You Will Need
> Comb and brush
> Chair
> Mirror
> Cup of water
> Smock or bath towel
> Optional: hair curlers, hairpins, ribbons, and scarves

What to Do
> **1.** Decide who will be the customer and who will be the barber.
> **2.** The customer says, "I need a new hairstyle."
> **3.** The barber says, "Sit right down."
> **4.** The barber tucks the smock or bath towel around the customer's neck, dips the comb and brush into the water, and restyles the customer's hair.
> **5.** The barber and the customer chat about the weather, their families, upcoming holidays, schools and playgrounds, and other neighborly news.
> **6.** Exchange roles.

Helpful Hints for Grown-ups
> • Some kids resist going to a barbershop to get their hair cut, but they may be more agreeable if you enact this little sociodramatic playlet before you go. Rehearsing a potentially scary experience is a psychologically sound practice.
> • Some kids resist getting their hair cut, period! You may have luck cutting a kid's hair yourself once your child is engrossed in the play and seated in the tight space of a "pretend" barber's chair.

CLASSROOM

Age Range: 6 and up, with help

What You Will Need
Blackboard, chalk, and eraser
Optional: chairs and desks

What to Do
   1. Decide who will be the teacher and who will be the student.
   2. The teacher says, "The lesson today is about farm animals (transportation, fractions, state capitals, spelling, etc.). Please go to the blackboard."
   3. The student makes a list of all the animals you can think of together, or works out problems, or writes answers to the teacher's questions.
   4. The teacher "corrects" the student's work or offers constructive comments about it.
   5. The teacher and the student exchange roles.

■ Secret Hideaway ■

Tight spaces are not always undesirable. A cozy, dark, secret space may be exactly what a child needs, especially when the weather outside is miserable or he is out of sorts.

Age Range: 3 to 7

What You Will Need
Large sheet, blanket, curtain, or canvas tarpaulin
Large safety pins (diaper pins are good), clothespins, or strapping tape

What to Do
   1. Choose a spot in your home for constructing a Secret Hideaway. This spot may be under the dining room table,

behind the living room couch, or in a corner of the bedroom.

2. Make a tent by attaching the sheet over the table or between a few pieces of sturdy furniture.

3. Furnish the hideaway with pillows, stuffed animals, and favorite toys.

4. Invite a friend to come in to pretend you are "desert isle kids."

5. If possible, leave the Secret Hideaway up for a day or two, until the sun comes out again.

Helpful Hints for Grown-ups

• Don't attach the sheet to standing lamps, because they are not stable.

• When your family gets a new appliance such as a refrigerator or washing machine, save that carton! With colorful markers, the child can draw an instrument panel for an imaginary spaceship or window boxes for a playhouse. With a sharp, pointed knife, a school-age child or an adult can cut windows and doors.

• Clear a closet for a short-term hideaway.

• Do you have bunk beds? Tuck the edges of sheets under the top mattress. Arrange the sheets outside the bed frame so that they hang to the floor like the walls of a tent.

"I'M ALL REVVED UP" OR "I'M TOO POOPED TO PLAY"

■

THE ACTIVITIES in this chapter differ from those in chapter 1 because on occasion, kids need something more. Being stuck indoors during a week of bad weather is an example of such an occasion.

When kids are restricted from playing vigorously and from handling bikes, balls, and playground equipment, they frequently react in one of two common ways.

One reaction is that they get sluggish. They can't seem to move. They have no pep to sustain normal activities and when they do shake themselves to get up and go, they fatigue easily. They are cranky and passive, and they behave inappropriately.

The second common reaction is that they get "wired." They can't sit still, even when quiet concentration is necessary. They can't pay attention to a parent or a teacher. They are fidgety, restless, and noisy. Irritable and overactive, they behave inappropriately too.

Whether kids respond to tight spaces by being sluggish or by getting wired, the reason is the same: They are missing opportunities to move and touch!

Kids gotta move and touch, just as much as birds gotta sing and fish gotta swim. When kids' bodies and brains are deprived of essential sensory experiences, they lose the ability to self-regulate.

Being self-regulated means being able to focus and to get

centered. In a perfect world, kids can arouse themselves from a sleepy state or calm themselves down from a state of excitement in order to function normally and in an organized way.

In a tight-space world, however, kids need help to find purposeful activities that will help them self-regulate. Some need activities to rev up; others need activities to slow down. They all need touch and movement experiences that will enable them to function smoothly throughout the day.

The multisensory activities in chapter 2 appeal to all kids—especially those who may have difficulty paying attention to the chapter 1 ideas. The purpose of these activities is to help kids get self-regulated, whether they are all revved up or too pooped to play.

The suggestions in this chapter are:

- Movement Activities
- Cooking and "Gooking" Activities
- Music and Sound Activities

MOVEMENT ACTIVITIES

Some kids are "bumpers-and-crashers." Craving sensory input from their muscles and movements, they seek vigorous activities as a kind of self-therapy to calm themselves down.

Other kids are "sleepyheads." They avoid vigorous play because they have low muscle tone or because they are not well coordinated.

The movement activities included in this section are fun and beneficial for every kid in a tight space.

- For exercising large body muscles, Pillow Crashing, The Feet-Beat Game, and the Back-to-Back Stand-Up Game are positively therapeutic.
- People Sandwich is an all-purpose, total-body activity that calms down a restless kid or stimulates a drowsy one.

- Rocking on a Teeter-totter will pull a kid together while improving his or her sense of balance.
- Ripping and Rolling Newspaper helps a kid develop upper body strength and coordination.

■ Pillow Crashing ■

To the kid who likes to jump on the bed, say, "Sure" instead of "No." After this activity, your child will feel better and calmer. On the other hand, maybe your kid lacks energy. Introduce this activity, and soon the child will go for it eagerly.

Age Range: 3 to 5, with help to get started

What You Will Need
Bed pillows
Couch cushions
Down comforters
Sleeping bags
Camp mattress

What the Grown-up Is to Do
1. Clear a spot in your home where bumping and crashing is okay. This may be a bedroom, the basement, or even the living room. Move lamps and breakable things out of the way.
2. Pile the pillows, cushions, comforters, etc., in a heap.
3. Let your kid take a running leap into the heap.

Helpful Hints for Grown-ups
- Drag a mattress from the bed to the floor and let the child jump on it.
- Better still, buy a small trampoline at a sporting goods store.

■ The Feet-Beat Game ■

A child's brain and whole body have a thoroughly good time by jumping to rhymes. This game provides a calming, up/down experience that improves sensorimotor skills, and helps the child to take in sensory information and respond in movement. Everybody can use this activity, which requires no more space than a small trampoline.

Age Range: 3 and up, with help to get started

What You Will Need
> Small trampoline (the kind used for aerobic exercise)
> Nursery rhymes, jump-rope chants, poems, and songs
> Rhythm instruments, such as rhythm sticks or tambourines

What to Do
> **1.** Choose a favorite rhyme or song. Here are some examples:
>> "The Eensy Weensy Spider"
>> "This Old Man, He Played One"
>> "Twinkle, Twinkle, Little Star" ("The Alphabet Song" and "Baa, Baa, Black Sheep" use the same tune)
>> "Jack and Jill"
>> "Miss Mary Mack"
>> "The Wheels on the Bus"
>> "Jingle Bells"
>> "Mary Had a Little Lamb"
>> "One, Two, Buckle My Shoe"
>> "Jack Sprat Could Eat No Fat"
>> "Jack Be Nimble, Jack Be Quick"
>> "Pease Porridge Hot"
>
> **2.** Or, choose a jump-rope chant, like one of these:

"MY FATHER IS A BUTCHER"

My father is a butcher,
My mother cuts the meat,
And I'm the little hot dog
Who runs around the street.

"TEDDY BEAR, TEDDY BEAR"

Teddy Bear, Teddy Bear, turn around,
Teddy Bear, Teddy Bear, touch the ground,
Teddy Bear, Teddy Bear, read the news,
Teddy Bear, Teddy Bear, tie your shoes,
Teddy Bear, Teddy Bear, go upstairs,
Teddy Bear, Teddy Bear, say your prayers,
Teddy Bear, Teddy Bear, turn off the light,
Teddy Bear, Teddy Bear, say good night!

"MISS LUCY HAD A BABY"

Miss Lucy had a baby,
His name was Tiny Tim,
She put him in the bathtub
To see if he could swim.

He drank up all the water,
He ate up all the soap,
He tried to eat the bathtub,
But it wouldn't go down his throat.

Miss Lucy called the doctor,
Miss Lucy called the nurse,
Miss Lucy called the lady
With the alligator purse.

In came the doctor,
In came the nurse,
In came the lady
With the alligator purse.

"Mumps," said the doctor,
"Measles," said the nurse,
"Nonsense," said the lady
With the alligator purse.

"Penicillin," said the doctor.
"Penicillin," said the nurse.
"Pizza!" said the lady
With the alligator purse.

A penny for the doctor,
A nickel for the nurse,
A dollar for the lady
With the alligator purse.

Out went the doctor,
Out went the nurse,
Out went the lady
With the alligator purse!

3. One person (or a group) recites or sings while beating a rhythm instrument or clapping rhythmically. Meanwhile, you jump to the beat. The game is to make your jumps match the fast or slow tempo of the spoken beat.
4. Next, decide how fast or slowly to jump. The person reciting the rhyme has to match the tempo of your feet-beat.
5. Take turns jumping and reciting—kids and grown-ups alike!

Variations
- Instead of chanting or singing, just count, one number for every bounce.
- Jump through the whole alphabet.
- Jump while you spell your name.
- Make up your own chants.

■　■　■

■ Back-to-Back Stand-Up Game ■

This game is for two or more restless kids. The game is easier for kids who have a lot of energy and firm muscle tone, but virtually any child will have fun giving it a try. This no-equipment activity is ideal for a tight space.

Age Range: 4 and up

What You Will Need
2 kids about the same size

What to Do
1. Sit on floor, back to back.
2. Link elbows.
3. Try to stand up without unlinking elbows.
4. Lower yourselves, again in one piece, to a sitting position. This is harder than it sounds!

Variations
• Try this game barefoot.
• Add another kid. A third body makes the game much more challenging and much more fun.

■ People Sandwich ■

Deep pressure is soothing for fidgety children (and for adults, too). This therapeutic activity takes up no more room than a bed, and it makes people laugh with pleasure.

Age Range: 3 and up, with help

What You Will Need
For the "sandwich bread," a gym mat works best, but you can also use a flexible mattress or a few large couch pillows.
For "spreaders," use a big sponge, a synthetic pot scrubber, a vegetable brush, a washcloth, and/or a butter-basting brush.

What the Grown-up Is to Do

1. Say, "Let's play People Sandwich. Want to be a salami or a turkey sandwich?" Have the child lie facedown on the "bread" (the gym mat or mattress), with her head extended beyond the edge.

2. Using differently textured spreaders, rub the child's arms, legs, and torso. Use firm strokes, as deep pressure is calming, but light tickles can be irritating. Say, "Now I'm spreading pretend relish (mayonnaise, ketchup, mustard, etc.) on this delicious sandwich."

3. Fold the gym mat over the child, making sure that her head is not covered. If you don't have a gym mat or mattress, cover her body with couch pillows. Say, "Here's the top slice of bread."

4. Say, "Too much relish! I need to squish some out." Press your hands firmly up and down the mat, so that the child underneath feels the pressure. "Squish, squish!"

5. Lie down on top of the gym mat. Roll or crawl over your child. You won't be too heavy, because the gym mat or pillows will distribute your weight. "Squish, squish!"

6. Remove the top slice of bread and make another People Sandwich, this time out of imaginary peanut butter, strawberry jam, marshmallows, etc. Your delighted child will have plenty of suggestions to keep the game going.

Helpful Hints for Grown-ups

• More than one child? Line them up side by side on the gym mat or mattress and make a "People Club Sandwich" with salami, turkey, roast beef, etc. The more the merrier.

• Want to know why kids ask to play People Sandwich? Get inside the sandwich yourself, and let your kid spread the relish and squish out the excess. You will *love* it!

■　■　■

■ Teeter-Totter ■

Back-and-forth movement, like the deep pressure of a People Sandwich, is also soothing for a kid who is rattling around the house.
    Back-and-forth, or "linear," movement includes:

- forward/backward motions (rocking in a rocking chair or swinging on a playground swing),
- up/down motions (bouncing on Grandpa's knee or jumping on a trampoline, as described in the next activity), and
- side-to-side motions (swaying in a cradle or a hammock).

This activity helps a kid "get it all together," with a simple piece of equipment that can be taken out anytime the walls seem to be closing in. After your child has spent a few minutes on a Teeter-Totter, you may notice improvements in balance, posture, and motor coordination, as well as in speech and attention.

Age Range: 3 and up

What You Will Need
    Block of wood about 2" × 4" × 12" for the base
    Board about 12" × 36"

What to Do
  1. Place the block of wood on a carpet.
  2. Center the board over the block.
  3. Stand on the board and tip from left to right.

Helpful Hints for Grown-ups
- Until kids get the hang of this, they may fall off the board, so make sure that no furniture is in the way.
- Do not put a cylinder under the board. A block is better because it prevents the board from slipping.

Variation

With a friend, use the Teeter-Totter as a miniature seesaw.

■ Ripping and Rolling Newspaper ■

Offer these simple and satisfying activities to a kid who has energy to spare and nowhere to spend it, as well as to a kid who could use a little jazzing up.

Ripping paper makes an interesting sound. Rolling paper makes a child feel useful. Both activities help develop a kid's large and small motor skills at the same time that they provide some innocent fun.

Age Range: 3 and up

What You Will Need

Heap of old newspapers
2 large paper bags

What to Do

1. Take 1 sheet of newspaper at a time and open it.

2. Rip the newspaper into strips.

3. Rip the strips into little pieces.

4. Make a mountain of ripped paper.

5. When you're tired of ripping, put all the pieces into a bag.

6. Here are some ideas for what you can do with ripped paper:

Recycling

Using in a package to protect something breakable

Lining the guinea pig's cage

Making a collage

Using a few pieces as streamers to decorate a Newspaper Hat

Pretending it is spaghetti (put some in a bowl and serve it to friends)

7. Take another sheet of newspaper, but keep this one folded. Lay it on the floor.

8. Starting at the narrow end, roll the newspaper as tightly as possible into the shape of a log.

9. Repeat with another newspaper sheet.

10. Put the newspaper logs into a bag and keep them near the fireplace for kindling.

Helpful Hint for Grown-ups

Ripping and Rolling Newspaper is dirty work, because the ink rubs off onto the kid's hands. Be sure that your child is wearing old clothes.

COOKING AND ''GOOKING'' ACTIVITIES

Some kids crave messy play, some kids shy away from it, and all kids need it. These hands-on recipes are for everybody:

- Smash Hit Cookies channel a kid's aggression, and they taste delicious, too.
- Oobleck, Stretchy Gook, and Homemade Playdough are made to order for the kid with nothing to do and nowhere to go. These activities are perfect for both revved-up and pooped-out kids.

■ Smash Hit Cookies ■

Sometimes a kid just wants to punch something. Pounding this dough provides a perfect outlet for tight-space aggression.

When these delicious cookies come out of the oven, they will be a smash hit!

Age Range: 4 to 7, with help
8 and up, without much help

What You Will Need to Make about 5 Dozen Cookies
   3 cups oatmeal
   1½ cups brown sugar
   1½ cups flour
   3 sticks butter or margarine, softened
   1½ teaspoons baking powder
   Cookie sheets

What to Do
   1. Dump all the ingredients into a large bowl. (Precise measuring is not important.)
   2. Smash, squeeze, mush, hit, punch, pinch, slap, and pummel the dough. The harder the pounding, the tastier the cookies.
   3. Roll the dough into small balls.
   4. Put the balls on ungreased cookie sheets.
   5. Bake the cookies at 350° for 10 minutes.
   6. Put them on a rack to cool (or eat them while they are still warm, if you can't wait).

Variation
   Add other ingredients, such as: raisins, chocolate chips, peanut butter chips, butterscotch chips, chopped nuts, chopped dates, dry cereal

■ Oobleck ■

Oobleck is a funny thing. You don't cook it, and you can't eat it, but it certainly is fun to play with.
   Try it; you'll like it.

Age Range: 4 and up (younger children will require help)

What You Will Need
   Water
   Measuring cup
   Box of cornstarch
   Optional: food coloring

What to Do
1. Put 1 cup of water into a large bowl.
2. Add 2 drops of food coloring, if you wish.
3. Slowly add the entire contents of the cornstarch box, stirring constantly.
4. If the mixture isn't smooth, add ¼ cup water. (Consistency depends on the amount of humidity in the air and the quality of the cornstarch.)
5. Stick one finger into the Oobleck. Your finger will go in easily.
6. Now, punch the Oobleck forcefully with your fist. Your fist will not penetrate, but will bounce back. Isn't that magic?

Helpful Hints for Grown-ups
* Leave Oobleck alone and it will separate into water and cornstarch again. By stirring vigorously, you can bring it back to life.
* You may refrigerate it for a week, after which it is wise to throw it away—into the trash can. Do not put it down the sink, because it will clog the drain.

Learning Value
Making Oobleck teaches kids about viscosity, which is the sticky, glutinous, slowly flowing quality of this crazy liquid.

■ Stretchy Gook ■

Here's some gloppy gook that is easy to make in a tight space and is quite interesting to play with. Kids love it and grownups don't mind it, because it doesn't stick to you.

Age Range: 3 to 7, with some help
8 and up, without much help

What You Will Need

2 tablespoons white glue
2 tablespoons laundry borax
¼ cup warm water
Paper cup

What to Do

1. Place the glue in the paper cup.
2. Dissolve the borax in the ¼ cup of warm water.
3. Add the borax liquid to the glue.
4. Stir and squeeze with your fingers until you have Stretchy Gook.
5. Roll the Stretchy Gook into a ball or a snake.
6. Pat it into a pancake, stretch it, snap it apart, squeeze it, bounce it, toss it in the air, and catch it.

■ Homemade Playdough ■

Playdough is a staple in the early-childhood classroom, and it certainly has value for use in every child's home. It is easy to make, fun to play with, and keeps well for another house-bound afternoon.

Age Range: 3 and up, with help

What You Will Need

Large cooking pot
Long handled-spoon
2 cups flour
1 cup salt
4 teaspoons cream of tartar
2 cups water
4 tablespoons vegetable oil
Food coloring

What to Do

1. Dump the flour, salt, cream of tartar, water, and oil into the cooking pot.

2. Stir, more or less constantly, over very low heat until the dough comes away from the edge of the pot and makes a soft ball.

3. When the playdough cools, add a few drops of food coloring. Blend in the coloring.

4. Use your hands to shape the playdough into pancakes, snakes, and balls.

5. Practice making letters, numbers, and shapes with the dough.

6. Use some of the things listed below to play with the dough:

> cookie cutters
> cookie molds
> rolling pin (or a cylindrical wooden block, or a short piece of a wooden dowel)
> scissors to cut it
> butter knife, fork, and spoon
> garlic press to make "spaghetti" or "hair" by squeezing the dough through the tiny holes
> egg slicer
> coins, keys, paper clips, plastic hair curlers, and other objects to make imprints in the playdough

Variations

• Add a few drops of peppermint extract or a teaspoon of cinnamon to give the playdough a pleasant smell.

• Substitute clay for playdough.

• Make Christmas tree decorations by forming shapes with cookie cutters. Poke a hole near the top of the shape so that you can put a ribbon through the hole after the decoration dries and hardens.

Helpful Hints for Grown-ups

• Don't worry if a small child eats some of the playdough. It won't taste very good, but it won't hurt him. If your

kid always seems to be putting inedible things into his mouth, give him a piece of chewing gum while he plays.
• Playdough won't stick to little fingers if you dust those little fingers with flour first.
• Store the playdough in an airtight cellophane bag or plastic container. It will remain soft and lovely to work with for weeks. If you have room to store it in the refrigerator, it will last even longer.
• Keep the playdough toys together and nearby so you won't have to go hunting for them the next time.

Learning Value

Helping to cook the Homemade Playdough teaches kids about measuring, mixing, and observing how ingredients change while they heat and cook.

MUSIC AND SOUND ACTIVITIES

Some kids have an innate interest in music and rhythm, while others need to be introduced gradually to some of life's greatest free pleasures. These are musical activities that will help release kids' pent-up energy or will arouse them to get moving and shaking:

• A Spoon Bell will intrigue every budding scientist/ musician when she hears its impressive "gong" ringing privately in her ears.
• Singing through a Kazoo gives kids a chance to sound off!
• Making an Oatmeal Box Drum, a Tin Can Bongo, a Flowerpot Timpani, and a Chopstick Mallet for a set of Homemade Drums will keep kids busy for quite a while.
• A Film Canister Shaker is a quiet percussion instrument that is easy to make and play.
• Playing a Talking String gives the ears a rest while other parts of the body get a workout.

■ Spoon Bell ■

Did you know that you can make a miniature Liberty Bell out of a spoon? When a metal object vibrates, it produces ringing tones.

This activity is simple—and not as noisy as you may think. A Spoon Bell makes a big, gonging sound to the person holding it, but a very quiet sound to everybody else.

The reason for the difference in loudness is that the vibrations traveling up the string are for the kid's ears only. Everyone else just hears a gentle tap when the spoon hits a hard object, and a loud *wow!* from the kid!

Age Range: 5 and up

What You Will Need
Metal tablespoon
3' length of string

What to Do
1. Tie the tablespoon to the middle of the string.
2. Wrap each of the loose ends of the string around the tips of your index fingers.
3. Stick your index fingers in your ears.
4. Lean forward, so that the spoon won't touch your body. (If it does touch your body or your clothes, the soft material will stop the vibrations that cause sound.)
5. Swing the spoon against the edge of a table. What do you hear? The Liberty Bell!
6. Roam around the room, swinging your Spoon Bell against chairs, flowerpots, walls, the posts of standing lamps, etc. Everything you hit with the Spoon Bell will produce a different sound.

Variations
• Make a Spoon Bell with a teaspoon. The smaller the spoon, the higher the sound. The bigger the spoon, the lower the sound.

• Weave some string through the bars of a cookie rack or an oven rack. Hold the ends of the strings to your ears and ask somebody else to strike the bars with a spoon. You will hear a weird and wonderful melody.

■ Kazoo ■

Every child is a born musician—even if he can't sing! Suggest this on a can't-sit-still-day.

But be prepared: This activity you will certainly hear!

Age Range: 4 and up, with minimum help

What You Will Need

Cardboard tube, such as a paper towel or toilet paper roll

Pencil

6" square of wax paper

Rubber band

What to Do

1. With the pencil, poke a hole into the cardboard tube, about 2" from the end. The hole will let the air out of the Kazoo when you blow into it.

2. Place the wax paper over the end nearest the hole.

3. Wrap the rubber band around the wax paper to keep it on the cardboard tube.

4. Sing "Old MacDonald Had a Farm" into the open end. The air escaping from your mouth will cause the paper to vibrate and make a buzzing sound. (Humming will not produce a buzzing sound. When you hum, you usually keep your mouth closed, and no air escapes.)

5. If the Kazoo doesn't buzz, try singing, "Ta, ta, ta, ta" instead of the words. If the Kazoo still doesn't buzz, loosen the wax paper a little bit. Sometimes the paper is just a little too tight and can't vibrate.

Variation

Did you know that you have your own built-in kazoo? It is your "Adam's apple." The Adam's apple is your larynx, or "voice box." It has a membrane that vibrates whenever air moves in your throat as you speak, hum, or sing. Put your fingertips on your Adam's apple and sing. Can you feel the membrane move? You can feel it best when you sing low notes.

Learning Value

Making and playing a Kazoo improves fine-motor skills, not only in the fingers and hands but also in the tongue and lips (important for speaking).

■ Homemade Drums ■

Kids in tight spaces normally express emotions of anger and aggression. Here are suggestions for making a few homemade rhythm instruments that will provide a positive outlet for all that pent-up frustration.

OATMEAL BOX DRUM

Age Range: 3 to 6, with help
7 and up, without help

What You Will Need

Cylindrical oatmeal box
Large nail
3' length of string
Masking tape
Pencil or Chopstick Mallet (see instructions page 116)

What to Do

1. To make a neck strap, take the nail and pierce small holes in opposite sides of the oatmeal box. The holes should be about 1" below the lid.

2. Remove the lid and press the ends of the string through the holes. Tie the string ends together inside the box.

3. Replace the lid and secure it to the box with tape.

4. Beat the drum with a pencil, a Chopstick Mallet, or your hands.

TIN CAN BONGO

Age Range: 3 to 6, with help
7 and up, without help

What You Will Need

3 tin cans of different sizes, such as a coffee can, a soup can, and a tuna fish can
Masking tape
Pencil or Chopstick Mallet (see instructions page 116)

What to Do

1. Place the cans side by side, upside down, with the opened ends facing up.

2. Strap the 3 cans together with tape. When the bongo is turned right side up, the drum heads will all be on the same plane, making it easier to play.

3. Beat out rhythms with your hand, a pencil, or a Chopstick Mallet.

Variation

Use 3 containers with plastic tops, such as those for coffee, cake frosting, and solid shortening. Put the cans side by side with their plastic lids down. Then tape the cans together.

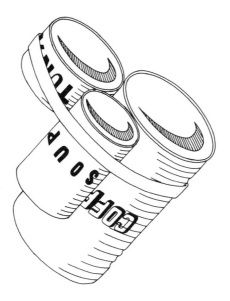

Helpful Hint for Grown-ups

For kids, plastic drumheads make a less satisfying sound than metallic drumheads, but for grown-ups, the softer sound may be more pleasant to listen to.

FLOWERPOT TIMPANI

Age Range: 3 to 6, with help
7 and up, without help

What You Will Need

3 large buttons
3 pieces of string, each about 12" long
3 flowerpots, each a different size
Dowel, about 3' long
Pencil or Chopstick Mallet (see instructions page 116)

What to Do

1. Thread a button on a piece of string.
2. Knot the string ends together.
3. Push the knot through the hole in a flowerpot so that the button is on the inside of the pot.
4. Prepare the second and third flower pots the same way.
5. Hang the pots, upside down, from the dowel.
6. Rest the ends of the dowel on the backs of two chairs.
7. Strike the pots with a mallet.

Helpful Hint for Grown-ups

Although the pots will have different tones, it will be difficult to find ones that will play any recognizable tunes! This instrument is more percussive than melodic.

CHOPSTICK MALLET

Age Range: 3 to 6, with help
7 and up, without help

What You Will Need

Cork
Large nail
White glue
Chopstick

What to Do

1. With the nail, make a hole in the small end of the cork.
2. Fill the hole with glue and push the end of the chopstick firmly into the gluey hole.
3. Let the glue dry.
4. When the glue is dry, beat the mallet on an Oatmeal Box Drum, Tin Can Bongo, or Flowerpot Timpani. (You can also use it for a Waterglass Xylophone, page 55.)

■ Film Canister Shaker ■

Like a Jingle-on-a-Stick (page 51), this homemade rhythm instrument is fun to make and shake, but the shaker requires less patience to prepare.

Age Range: 3 and up

What You Will Need
2 plastic film canisters
Dried beans, rice, buttons, or pebbles
Masking tape

What to Do
1. Put about 10 dried beans or other small, hard objects into each of the 2 empty film canisters.
2. Snap the lids onto the canisters.
3. Join the canisters bottom to bottom with masking tape.

Variations
• To make a simpler shaker, use just 1 film canister.
• To make a slightly louder shaker, use 3 film canisters and tape them together in a long row.
• Experiment with different kinds of containers. A bigger, plastic container will make a louder, lower sound. A metal container will make a really loud noise, but maybe that is not such a good idea when you're in a tight space!

Helpful Hints for Grown-ups
• The shaker will sound best with only a few beans in each canister. A few beans have space to rattle around and make a shaking noise, but a lot of beans crowded into a tight space can't move or make a sound.
• Be prepared for your child to ignore your explanation and to fill the canisters to the brim. That's okay. Remem-

ber, children need to DO in order to understand. By all means, *let your kid experiment.*

• You may want to glue or tape lids shut to prevent small children from opening the canisters.

■ Talking String ■

Making and playing a Talking String is a multisensory activity that encourages kids to concentrate and to use many body parts simultaneously. The activity helps to calm a revved-up kid and to arouse a pooped-out kid.

Soon, your kid will have a whole homemade band—and plenty to do in a tight space!

Age Range: 4 and up, with help

What You Will Need
3' length of 30-pound fishing line
Flat piece of wood, about 8" long
Large wooden bead

What to Do
1. Tie one end of the fishline around the center of the wood.
2. Attach the bead to the other end of the fishline.
3. Step on the wood.
4. Pull the bead with one hand and strum the fishline string with the other hand.
5. Pull the string hard to make the sound of the string higher. (The sound will be higher because a tight string causes fast vibrations and a high musical pitch.)
6. Now pull the string gently to make the sound lower. (The sound will be lower because a loose string causes slow vibrations and a low musical pitch.)
7. Imitate a conversation between a Tadpole and a Daddy Frog, or between Goldilocks and the Biggest Bear.

Learning Value

Playing a Talking String is good for the whole body:

* Using one foot to stabilize the wood base, one hand to hold the wooden bead, and the other hand to pluck the string improves motor coordination among different parts of the body.
* Stretching and relaxing the string teaches about how much physical force is necessary to control its tension.
* Plucking the string strengthens fine-motor control in the fingers and hand.
* Producing high sounds and low sounds develops auditory discrimination.

"I FEEL YUCKY ALL OVER"

(S I C K I N B E D)

■

QUESTION: WHAT makes a kid more irritable than feeling sick?
Answer: Feeling better!

When a kid gets sick enough to have to go to bed, nursing the child back to health is a parent's first concern. When you're worried about lowering a fever, soothing a rash, or making it easier for your kid to breathe, fun and entertaining activities may be the last thing on your mind.

But when a child begins to get better, she gets restless. She insists that she is well enough to get out of bed, out of the house, and back to school, even though she needs more time to recover.

Now is the time to introduce some quiet-time activities that will keep an under-the-weather, lonely kid amused, without draining her energy. The suggestions in this chapter include:

- Cutting Magazines and Catalogs to find appealing pictures, and pasting the pictures into a Favorite Things Scrapbook
- Three peaceful Stringing Projects: Stringing Buttons, Stringing with Pipe Cleaners, and Stringing Macaroni
- Hanging objects on a dowel to produce soothing Musical Metal Wind Chimes

- Flour Sifting, a simple and pleasant hands-on activity
- Making up stories and rearranging felt shapes in Felt Board Fun
- Doing nothing at all except watching flowers change color as they absorb water dyed with food coloring (Coloring Flowers)

It is not necessary to restrict these quiet activities to days when a kid is sick. Try them at other times as well.

■ Cutting Magazines and Catalogs ■

Cutting pictures out of magazines and catalogs is a peaceful activity for a child who is confined to bed.

Age Range: 4 and up

What You Will Need
Stack of old magazines and catalogs
Scissors
Paper
Markers
Glue
Large envelopes
Optional: scrapbook

What to Do
1. Look through the pages and cut out interesting pictures, like:
Animals, such as mammals, fish, birds, and reptiles
Insects and spiders
Flowers, trees, and plants
Weather scenes, such as snow, rain, lightning, clouds
Summer, fall, winter, and spring scenes
Planets, stars, and comets
Movie stars
Cartoon characters

Body parts, such as arms, legs, eyes, mouths, ears, etc.

Toys

Appliances, such as computers, telephones, washing machines, and stoves

Household objects, such as furniture, flashlights, dog dishes, coffeepots, and silverware

Sporting equipment, such as skates, skis, fishing rods, baseball bats, tennis rackets, and basketballs

Food, such as vegetables, fruits, breads and cereals, meats, dairy products, and desserts

Cars, trains, trucks, airplanes

Words and sentences

Objects beginning with the letter *B* or *D,* etc.

2. Glue the pictures onto paper:

Put together a crazy face or funny person from the mixed-up body parts

Tell a story in pictures

Use cutout words for a mysterious message, such as, *"**Give** UP the **cookies** Right **NOW!**"*

3. When the glue is dry, the papers can decorate the bedroom walls or go into a Favorite Things Scrapbook (see the next activity).

4. Group unused pictures together and put the best ones into the envelopes. Label the envelopes "Animals," "Face Parts," etc. You can use these later for collages or other projects.

■ Favorite Things Scrapbook ■

Positive thinking is what a kid needs most when all he can do is think about how lousy he feels. It really does help brighten one's outlook on life to "think lovely thoughts," as Peter Pan would say. This activity gets a young child's mind off his aches and itches, and it can be done while recuperating in bed.

Age Range: 4 and up

What You Will Need
Pictures cut from old magazines and catalogs
Typing paper punched with 3 holes
Glue
Adhesive tape
Scissors
Markers or crayons
3-ring binder or scrapbook

What to Do
1. Stick pictures of your favorite things on pieces of paper. On each page, you may want to put just a few pictures or a lot of pictures.
2. Write a few words about your pictures, like "Toys I Like to Play With," or "Zoo Animals." Or ask someone to help write what you want to say.
3. Put the pages into a 3-ring binder or scrapbook.

Variations
• Make an All About Me Scrapbook. One page may have pictures of the beach, like the beach where your family goes in the summer. Other pages may have pictures of toys or clothes like the ones you own. If you can't find pictures to cut out from magazines, you can draw them.
• Make a Future Family Scrapbook. Cut out pictures of people and things that you would like to have in your family when you grow up. These pictures may include:
yourself
husband or wife
children
pets
friends
clothes
house
furniture

Some of the scrapbook pages could have flip-up pictures. For instance, you could paste clothes on top of the people—first underwear, then shorts, then dresses or slacks, etc. You could also paste down an arrangement of furniture and then paste a house on top. Flip up the top picture to see what's underneath.

Write descriptions under the pictures, such as, "This is my daughter, Amy. These are her clothes." (Use a pencil so you can change the descriptions.)

Helpful Hint for Grown-ups

A Favorite Things Scrapbook will become an heirloom one day. Store it in the child's Memory Box for the kid to take out and admire on another tight-space occasion.

■ Stringing Projects ■

Here is a string of soothing and easy activities for the kid who is not feeling well and is stuck in bed.

STRINGING BUTTONS

Age Range: 3 to 6 (some children will need help to prepare the strings, but even the youngest will be able to do the stringing without any assistance)

What You Will Need

Lots of buttons
Dental floss or embroidery floss
Tapestry needle

What to Do

1. Cut a piece of dental floss about 2' long.
2. Thread the floss on the tapestry needle (you may need help to do this).
3. Thread the needle and floss through the first button.

4. Tie one end of the floss to the button so it won't slide off.

5. String on more buttons. Leave about 5" or 6" of the floss free so that there will be enough left over to tie the ends together.

6. Tie the ends together to make a pretty necklace.

Helpful Hints for Grown-ups

• Even when kids don't feel well enough to do a stringing project, buttons are pleasant to scoop up and sift through the fingers.

• No buttons around the house? You can buy a bagful at a sewing shop, variety store, hobby shop, or even the grocery store.

• No dental floss, no embroidery floss, and no tapestry needle? You could also use string or yarn, prepared in this way:

Dip 1" of the end of the yarn end into white glue.

Rest the end on wax paper. When it dries, it will be firm enough to stick through the button holes.

• This activity is not appropriate for children who still tend to put small, inedible objects into their mouths.

STRINGING WITH PIPE CLEANERS

Age Range: 4 and up

What You Will Need

Scissors
Scraps of construction paper
Hole puncher
About 10 drinking straws
About 30 pipe cleaners

What to Do

1. Cut construction paper scraps into small shapes, such as squares and triangles. The shapes should be about 1" or 2" in size.

2. Punch a hole in each shape.

3. Cut drinking straws into 2" pieces.

4. String a paper square or triangle onto a pipe cleaner.

5. Stick the tip of the pipe cleaner into a straw piece.

6. Stick the tip of a second pipe cleaner into the other end of the straw piece. Now you will have 2 pipe cleaners connected by 1 straw piece. The pipe cleaner tips will fit snugly inside the straws and will stay in place.

7. String a paper shape onto the second pipe cleaner.

8. Add another straw connector, another pipe cleaner, and another paper shape. Keep going until you have a big construction.

9. Bend the pipe cleaners into interesting angles.

STRINGING MACARONI

Age Range: 3 to 6

What You Will Need
Dry macaroni with holes, such as:
 wheels
 rotini
 rigatoni
 ziti
 penne
Markers
Yarn or string
Scissors
Cellophane tape

What to Do
1. Decorate the macaroni pieces with markers.

2. Cut a length of yarn about 2' long.

3. Wrap cellophane tape around one end of the yarn to make the end go through the macaroni easily.

4. String the macaroni on the yarn.

5. Tie the ends of the yarn together to make a colorful necklace.

Variations of Stringing Projects

* Use fishing line as the string.
* Use a shoelace.
* Make bracelets or Christmas tree ornaments.
* String dry cereal (the kind with holes) to make a beautiful and delicious necklace.
* String a variety of buttons, beads, sequins, straw sections, macaroni, and cereal to make an interesting pattern. Repeat the pattern several times on the same string.

Learning Value

Stringing Projects improve visual sequencing, which is the ability to understand logical order and to follow patterns.

■ Musical Metal Wind Chimes ■

This is a peaceful activity that results in a peaceful product.

Age Range: 3 and up, with help

What You Will Need

Variety of metal objects, such as:
    blunt-tipped screws
    nuts and bolts
    drawer pulls
    door hinges
    spoons and forks
    keys
    blunt-tipped scissors
    kitchen gadgets
Colorful yarn cut into 12" lengths
Tree branch or wooden dowel, about 3' long

What to Do
1. Tie a loop of yarn to each object.
2. Thread the loops onto the branch, about 3" apart.
3. Suspend the branch between the backs of 2 chairs and run a spoon from left to right across the dangling objects. When they hit one another, they make a soothing, tinkling sound.
4. Hang the branch near a window or from a tree outside for the wind to play.

Helpful Hints for Grown-ups
- Adult supervision is necessary because tying the yarn on the metal objects requires some skill.
- Do this activity on the rug, not in the bed.

Learning Value
Making Musical Metal Wind Chimes:

- improves bilateral coordination when the child uses both hands together to open the loop of yarn in order to get it around the branch,
- develops motor planning when the child has to figure out how to string the objects onto the branch, and
- teaches the child about vibrations when she runs a spoon across the row of dangling objects to make them hit one another.

■ Flour Sifting ■

Don't laugh! Sifting flour requires very little effort from a kid who is not feeling very strong, yet wants to do something besides lie in bed and mope. Furthermore, this activity is enormously satisfying and soothing.

Age Range: 3 and up

What You Will Need

Newspaper

Flour sifter (a squeeze handle is excellent for developing fine-motor muscles in the hand and fingers; a turn handle is easier to manipulate and may be better for a sick child)

Measuring cup or large spoon

Square sheets of wax paper

Flour in a bag, canister, or bowl

What to Do

1. Spread newspaper on the kitchen floor.

2. Set down the flour sifter, measuring cup or spoon, squares of wax paper, and flour.

3. Scoop flour into the sifter.

4. Sift the flour over the wax paper. Make a little mountain. Touch it (but don't eat it).

5. Bring together opposite sides of the wax paper to make a chute for the flour.

6. Slide the flour back into the sifter, and sift it again.

Variations

• Sift different kinds of flour, such as whole wheat or rye.

• Instead of sifting flour, separate sand and pebbles.

• Spread glue in a design on a piece of paper and sift flour or sand onto the design.

Helpful Hint for Grown-ups

If the kid is *really sick* with a contagious disease, don't use the flour for cooking, and wash the sifter well.

■ Coloring Flowers ■

Nothing happens fast for a kid recuperating from an illness. Why not give him something to watch that happens slowly but surely—just as he will get better, slowly but surely? Besides being interesting to watch, the flowers will give off a delicate fragrance in the child's room.

Age Range: 3 and up

What You Will Need
    3 white carnations or daisies
    3 tall water glasses
    3 bottles of food coloring

What to Do
    1. Fill the glasses about halfway with water.
    2. Add a few drops of red food coloring to one glass, green to another, and blue to the third.
    3. Put 1 flower into each glass.
    4. Watch the flowers "drink" the colored water and become red, green, or blue. (This will take a few hours to happen.)

Variation
Put celery into the colored water.

■ Felt Board Fun ■

A felt board is a rectangular piece of heavy cardboard (or lightweight plywood) that is covered with felt or flannel. Shapes, letters, and figures that have been cut out of smaller pieces of felt or flannel will stick to the board. Children can easily arrange and rearrange the pieces to tell stories, make interesting designs, and spell words. This is a simple toy to make, and it will provide hours of quiet entertainment for a sick-in-bed kid.

Age Range: 3 to 7 (an adult's help will be necessary to make a felt board, but kids enjoy playing with one without any help at all)

What You Will Need

Rectangular piece of sturdy cardboard or lightweight plywood, about 18" × 24"

Rectangular piece of beige, light blue, or gray felt (about 24" by 30") for covering the board

Soft lead pencil

Scissors

Masking or strapping tape

Pieces of colored felt, wool, or flannel, for cutting up into shapes, letters, etc.

Coffee can or shoe box

What to Do

1. Center the cardboard or plywood on the felt rectangle. Pull up the edges of the felt, and tape them to the board.

2. With the pencil, make sketches onto the other pieces of colored felt of shapes and figures, such as:

Circles, half-circles, squares, triangles, rectangles, trapezoids, hexagons, octagons, rhomboids, etc.

Numbers

Letters

Body parts (eyes, mouths, heads, arms, etc.)

People and animals

Furniture (tables, beds, chairs, etc.)

3. Cut out the penciled shapes.

4. Stick the shapes on the felt board:

To tell stories

To build houses

To put together faces and bodies

To count or match circles and triangles

To count out numbers

To line up letters of the alphabet

To spell out words

To make pretty designs

5. Store the shapes in the can or box.

Learning Value

Manipulating the felt pieces:

* gives kids tactile and kinesthetic lessons about shapes, letters, and numbers, and
* encourages kids to use imagination to make up stories.

"WHEN ARE WE GOING TO GET THERE?"

(CAR, TRAIN, AND PLANE TRIPS)

■

TRAVELING WITH little children is not particularly pleasant. Who ever said that getting there was half the fun? It couldn't have been anyone with kids.

Still, the beach beckons, or the mountains call, or devoted grandparents are waiting to embrace you. Getting there can't be as bad as staying home all summer in town, right?

Indeed, while a family vacation has many excellent points, getting there is not going to be remembered as one of them. Traveling with children is a challenge even for parents who are incredibly patient, well rested, and creative, and who feels like that while on the road?

The ideas in this chapter may help you and the kids actually enjoy the trip. When you try some of the suggestions, maybe you *will* feel patient, well rested, and creative—and maybe you will find that getting there isn't half bad.

The ideas in this chapter include:

- A Busy Box and Trip Tapes, two quiet activities to pass the time while strapped in a seat
- Ojos de Dios and Pipe Cleaner Garlands, two easy "art" projects
- Three paper-and-pencil games: Fifty States License Plates Game, Highway Scavenger Hunt, and Memory Booster
- Three family games that require no equipment: Road

Sign Alphabet, Grandmother's Trunk, and Apples are Red

• Joint Squeeze, a tight-space exercise for travel-weary bones

■ Busy Box ■

To while away weary hours on the road, every kid needs a personal toy box filled with treasures.

Age Range: 3 and up

What You Will Need
Sturdy cardboard box
Tiny cars
Pencils, washable markers, crayons
Fresh pad of paper, coloring books
Pipe cleaners
Dollhouse people or action figures
Pegboard games

What to Do
1. Before setting out, prepare the Busy Box.
2. On the road, get busy and have a good time!

Helpful Hints for Grown-ups
• Avoid anything sharp, noisy, or smelly—for your child's sake as well as your own.
• Place a tray upon a few duffel bags or pillows on the seat next to or between the children. A tray makes a fine table for rolling little cars, and it doubles nicely as a physical barrier. As a rule, the greater the distance between children, the more pleasant the journey.
• Present small, wrapped gifts to the children *when they are being good.* Given at the right time, a new toy reinforces appropriate behavior; given at the wrong time, it teaches children that misbehavior pays.

■ Trip Tapes ■

Buying a portable cassette recorder/player designed specifically for children is an expenditure worth making before going on a trip. At about the age of three, a child may be able to operate one alone.

Age Range: 3 and up

What You Will Need

> Several prerecorded audio tapes, especially those that are entertaining, educational, and pleasant to listen to repeatedly
>
> Blank tapes for the kids to record their own songs or to describe what they see on the trip
>
> Box to keep the tapes and cassette recorder in

What a Grown-up Is to Do (Before You Leave on Your Trip)

1. Record your own tapes. The most soothing sound to a young child is your voice, whether you are singing songs or telling stories. These stories may be favorite bedtime stories or fairy tales that you read from storybooks.

2. If you choose to record a story from a picture book, ring a bell near the microphone when it is time to turn the page. Then, with the tape recorder running and the book in hand, a three- or four-year-old may be able to "read" along as she listens to the tape and turns the book's pages at the sound of the bell.

3. Record the child's voice and sound effects, too. It's fun for children to hear themselves moo and oink and make mysterious sounds. You will find that homemade tapes are worth the effort.

Helpful Hints for Grown-ups
- Bring plenty of extra batteries.
- Earphones for the child are a worthwhile purchase if you would rather not listen to the songs or stories for the umpteenth time. Be sure to check the volume on your kid's earphones, as loud noises can damage a child's hearing. If you can hear the songs from the front seat of the car, then the volume is probably too high.

■ Ojos de Dios ■

Ojos de Dios (pronounced "oh-hos day dee-os") means Eyes of God in Spanish. Weaving these lovely yarn diamonds is a peaceful, open-ended activity. Each one is beautiful, no matter what pattern or size a kid chooses.

Age Range: 6 and up

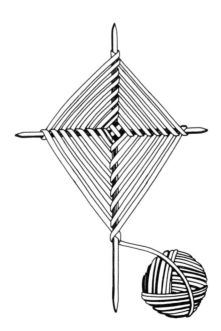

What You Will Need

2 sticks (twigs, craft sticks, chopsticks, etc.)
Yarn of different colors

What to Do

1. Cross 1 stick on top of the other to make 4 arms.

2. Crisscross a piece of yarn over the intersection several times to keep the sticks together.

3. Wrap yarn once around each arm, going over it and under it, and then bring the yarn to the next arm. Continue wrapping the yarn over and under each arm to form a diamond pattern.

4. Change colors when you feel like it. When you change to a new color, you may tie the ends of the yarn together, but you don't really have to. Just tuck the ends in. As you continue working, the ends will get "locked" into place.

5. Tie the last end of yarn so that it won't unravel.

■ Pipe Cleaner Garland ■

A few packages of pipe cleaners will quietly entertain a child for a long time.

Age Range: 3 and up

What You Will Need

A few packages of different-colored pipe cleaners

What to Do

1. Twist the ends of 1 pipe cleaner together to make a circle.

2. Put one end of a second pipe cleaner through the circle and twist its ends together to make a second circle.

3. Keep adding pipe cleaner circles.

4. Connect the first and last circle to make a circle of circles.

■ Fifty States License Plates Game ■

How many different license plates can a kid spot on passing cars? If your highway trip is long enough, he may "collect" licenses from all fifty states—even Hawaii.

Fifty States License Plates Game is not just entertaining; it is also educational. While the child is occupied with the search, he is getting lessons in geography and spelling.

The game is even more enjoyable when the whole family joins in. As children grow, they will especially remember activities you have done together as a family and they will pass them on when their own kids are fidgeting in the backseat.

Age Range: 6 and up

What You Will Need
Pencil
Stack of 3" × 5" note cards

What to Do
1. Write the state's name on a separate card each time you see a different license plate.
2. Keep the cards in your Busy Box (page 134).

Variations
• Put the cards in alphabetical order.
• Group the cards into regions, such as:
New England States
Midwest States
States East of the Mississippi River
States Bordering the Atlantic Ocean
• Search for license plates from foreign countries.
• Collect funny vanity plates, such as GRANDMA, ILUVYOU, or THNKSNW.
• Think up a vanity plate of your own, using 7 or fewer letters. If your name is Jonathan, your vanity plate might say, JONATHN. If you like gymnastics, your plate

might say, GYMNAST. What do you want people to know about you?

■ Road Sign Alphabet ■

Here is another activity to pass the time on a long car trip. Even preschoolers can play if they are able to recognize letters.

Age Range: 6 and up

What You Will Need
Sharp eyes
Knowledge of "The Alphabet Song"

What to Do
1. Spot and call out the letters of the alphabet, in order, as you see them. Look for them:
on highway and street signs
on billboards
on storefronts
on motel and movie marquees
2. Stop when you have found *Z*.

Helpful Hint for Grown-ups
A child can play this game alone, although it is much more fun to do it with others. Younger children enjoy playing as team members, contributing letters to the alphabet when they see them. Older children prefer to compete, racing against siblings and parents to build their own alphabet. The prize is the satisfaction of completing the alphabet first.

■ Highway Scavenger Hunt ■

Need another game to occupy kids in the backseat? A Highway Scavenger Hunt may be just the ticket.

Age Range: 4 and up

What You Will Need
   A list of things one typically spots on the highway. The
list may include:
   City Sights:
      smokestack
      department store
      grocery store
      used car lot
      penthouse
      radio tower
      stadium
      statue
      fountain
      school
      playground
   Suburban Sights:
      swimming pool
      park
      bike path
      shopping center
   Farmland Sights:
      barn
      silo
      stone wall
      pond
      cornfield
      tractor
      bale of hay
      corral
      horses and cows
      ducks and geese
   Wilderness Sights:
      river
      mountain
      lake

island
split-log fence
tent
campfire
person fishing
jeep

What to Do

1. Search for the things that are on the list.
2. Check the things off the list.

Variations

This game is not limited to traveling by automobile. You may also enjoy:

- Train Scavenger Hunt
  clock
  words like *No Smoking, Coach,* and *Club Car*
  freight car
  signaling lights
  man carrying a bouquet of flowers
  woman in a yellow blouse
  kid in a Redskins cap
- Airport/Airplane Scavenger Hunt
  carrying box for a dog or cat
  skycap
  Duty-Free shop
  someone with a sunburn
  someone wearing sandals with socks
  someone in a leg cast with skis strapped to his back

Helpful Hint for Grown-ups

Each child can have an individual copy of the list, or you can use one master list. If you have a few minutes before departure time, brainstorm with the children. Otherwise, make a list together once you are all settled in the car, train, or plane and the journey has begun.

■ Grandmother's Trunk ■

This memory game is as old as Grandmother! The kids can play it in the backseat, or you all can play it as a family game. Don't be surprised if the kids have better memories than you.

Age Range: 4 and up

What to Do

1. The first player thinks of an object to put in a make-believe trunk. The object can be something that is really useful for a trip or something funny. For example, the first player may say, "Grandmother has a walkie-talkie in her trunk."

2. The second player repeats what the first player put in and adds something else. For instance, "Grandmother has a walkie-talkie and a snakeskin in her trunk."

3. The third player says, "Grandmother has a walkie-talkie, a snakeskin, and a jar of peanut butter in her trunk."

4. The game ends when somebody gets the order mixed up or leaves something out.

Variations

• Think of objects in alphabetical order, such as "an apple pie, a Bible, a corncob pipe, and a dog leash."

• Think of things that get bigger and bigger, such as "a poppy seed, an ant, a cricket, a bird, . . . Mt. Everest!"

• Think of things that rhyme, such as: "a bee, a tree, a sea, a marquee, and a flea."

• Decide on a specific category of objects, such as:
  Tools and gadgets Grandmother uses in the kitchen
  Kinds of flowers that grow in the spring
  Supplies needed for a trip to the moon

■ Memory Booster ■

Remembering facts is easy when you play the entertaining and educational Memory Booster game, using *rhymes, acronyms,* or *mnemonics.*

Rhymes remind us of facts like historical dates ("In 1492, Columbus sailed the ocean blue"), days of the months ("Thirty days hath September, April, June, and November"), and spelling rules ("i before e, except after c"). Singing "Papa Haydn wrote this tune, on a sunny afternoon" to the familiar tune of the "Surprise" Symphony helps us remember the name of its composer, Franz Joseph Haydn.

Acronyms are new words made up of the first letters of a series of words, such as SCUBA (Self-Contained Underwater Breathing Apparatus) or WAC (Women's Army Corps). While HOMES is not a made-up word, it is a kind of acronym for the Great Lakes: Huron, Ontario, Michigan, Erie, and Superior.

Mnemonics (pronounced "nee-MA-nics") is the art of memory development that uses sentences to help us remember facts in a particular order. Mnemonics is a practice named for Mnemósyne, the Greek goddess of memory and the mother of the Muses. (The word *mnemon* means "mindful.")

Here are some examples of mnemonics:

• Musical syllables: Rodgers and Hammerstein's Doe, a Deer, a Female Deer; Ray, a Drop of Golden Sun, etc. (Do, Re, Mi, Fa, So, La, Ti, Do)
• Musical notes on the lines of the treble clef staff: Every Good Boy (or Beginner) Does Fine (E, G, B, D, F)
• Rainbow colors: ROY-G-BIV (Red, Orange, Yellow, Green, Blue, Indigo, Violet)
• Biology's classification system: King Philip Came Over For Gene's Special Variety (Kingdom, Phylum, Class, Order, Family, Genus, Species, Variety)
• Planets in order of distance from the sun: My

Very Elegant Mother Just Served Us Nine Pizzas (Mercury, Venus, Earth, Mars, Jupiter, Saturn, Uranus, Neptune, Pluto)
• First five books of the Bible: Green Elephants Love Nourishing Doughnuts (Genesis, Exodus, Leviticus, Numbers, Deuteronomy)
• United States presidents (1st to 11th): When A Just Man Makes A Just Vow, He Takes Pains (Washington, John Adams, Jefferson, Madison, Monroe, John Quincy Adams, Jackson, Van Buren, Harrison, Tyler, Polk)
• United States presidents (12th to 18th): The Foolish People Beheaded Lady Jane Grey (Taylor, Fillmore, Pierce, Buchanan, Lincoln, Andrew Johnson, Grant)

Age Range: 8 and up

What You Will Need
Paper and pencil
Almanac, pocket atlas, or road map

What to Do
1. Choose a category of facts you want to remember, such as:
    The seven dwarfs in Disney's version of *Snow White*
    Santa's reindeer
    The first thirteen United States colonies
    National parks your family has visited
    The continents
    The oceans
    Sports facts
    Metric system prefixes
2. Brainstorm with your family to make a list of the items in your chosen category, and write the words in a column down the left side of your paper.
3. Use the first letters of the words to make up a rhyme, acronym, or mnemonic to tie all the items together, like this:

> New England States
>
> | | |
> |---|---|
> | Maine | My |
> | Vermont | Very |
> | New Hampshire | Neat |
> | Massachusetts | Mother |
> | Rhode Island | Really |
> | Connecticut | Cares! |

■ Apples Are Red ■

Apples Are Red is a game of associations. Making associations helps us learn. For instance, a toddler sees a picture of a lion and says, "Meow!" because she associates the animal with her family cat.

A kindergartner, learning about shapes, recognizes triangles and octagons by associating them with Yield and Stop signs.

And a parent associates crumbs on a child's face with an empty cookie jar!

A kid's ability to connect bits of knowledge grows with time and practice. Apples Are Red is a game that greases the skids for developing this crucial learning skill.

Age Range: 3 and up, with an adult or another child

What to Do

1. The game is to listen to another person's statement and to respond to it with an associated, or similar, idea. The game starts and ends with the same statement. The player who gets back to the original sentence wins the game. To begin, the first player says a sentence.

2. The second player responds with a related idea.

3. The game continues until a player can return logically to the first sentence. Here's an example:

"Apples are red."
"Red is the color of fire engines."
"A fire engine needs a hose."
"A hose carries water."
"Water makes raindrops."
"Raindrops make rainbows."
"Rainbows come out in the sunshine."
"Sunshine makes it fun to play outside."
"We play outside in the backyard."
"The backyard has a garden."
"The garden has tomatoes."
"Tomatoes are red."
"Apples are red!"

3. Now the second player gets to go first by suggesting a new thought.

Helpful Hints for Grown-ups

• When you play Apples Are Red, remember to use words that refer to objects and events with which children are familiar. Then the child will be able to make an age-appropriate response. In other words, when you're playing this game with a preschooler, offer a statement about something in her frame of reference, like apples, rather than pomegranates.

• As a rule, very young children are likely to refer to objects that move, like fire engines. As kids mature and become more experienced, their vocabularies will develop to include complex and abstract terms, like "catastrophe."

• Because you are a parent, you can't avoid wanting to improve your kid's vocabulary and cognitive abilities. That is as it should be, but just don't make this game too difficult by introducing words that are so challenging that the child doesn't know how to respond. Keep in mind that Apples Are Red is supposed to be fun, so that the kid in a tight space feels happy and successful.

Variations

Instead of bringing the Apples Are Red full circle, all the way back to the original word, you could also just make a long list of people, objects, or ideas. Examples might be:

- People named Tom, Tommy, or Thomas (Tom Thumb, Tom Sawyer, Tommy in the third grade with the freckles, Tommy Tune, St. Thomas, Thomas Edison . . .)
- Things that you remember about Aunt Rose (her delicious angel's food cake, her dog with all those puppies, the stone rabbit in her garden, her "magic" yellow soap to prevent poison ivy, her old-world lullabies, the whiskers on her chin . . .)

■ **Joint Squeeze** ■

Kids have a particularly hard time sitting still for long periods because Nature's plan is for them to feel continual sensations of movement from their muscles and joints. Here's something you can do to provide sensory input for the kid who is about to explode out of the airplane seat belt.

Age Range: any age, with help

What to Do

1. Put one hand on your kid's forearm and another hand on his upper arm. With slow, firm pressure, push his forearm and his upper arm together, toward the elbow.
2. Now gently pull his forearm and his upper arm away from the elbow.
3. Repeat the pushing and pulling action several times.
4. "Squeeze" the other elbow.
5. Squeeze shoulders, knees, and ankles.
6. With both hands, push down on the kid's head. The pressure he feels in his skull, neck, and shoulders is soothing.

Helpful Hints for Grown-ups

• This is a technique that occupational therapists use to stimulate a person's ability to know where his body parts are and what they are doing. The more a person moves, the more he receives essential sensory information from his muscles and joints. When kids are prevented from moving, they are not getting this information, and that's why they're stir-crazy.

• Teach your child how to squeeze his own knees, ankles, and neck joints.

Variation

Joint Stretch:

• Take off your shoes and, while you count to five, stretch your toes as wide apart as you can. This is called *extension.*

• Now, count to five again and slowly scrunch up your toes. This is called *flexion.*

• Move up your body, to your ankles, knees, waist, and all the way to your fingers. Extend and flex each joint while you count to five. By the time you're done stretching all the joints that you can find, you'll feel lots better.

"I WANT TO GO HOME!"

(DOCTOR'S OFFICE, GROCERY STORE, WAITING IN LINE)

■

ONE MINUTE in a doctor's office is one minute too long for most kids. Waiting in line is also intolerable, whether the wait happens at the supermarket checkout counter, at the bus stop, or in front of the movie theater.

Pleading with kids to "hush up," or to "be patient for just another few minutes," or to "stop clinging and whining" never seems very successful. The reason is that kids need to be distracted from the boredom of waiting, and we often make the mistake of reminding them, instead.

One day at the grocery store, I stood behind a harried mother and her lively four-year-old who was earnestly trying to get out of the grocery cart's seat. The mother was saying, "You have to be patient for another few minutes. Oh, this is taking so long. We'll never get out of here. Sit down! This instant! You've got to be patient. I'll spank you if you're not patient!"

The child closed his eyes and covered his ears while she spoke. Then he opened his eyes and said with a sigh, "Mommy, you are patienting me to *death.*"

This chapter includes suggestions for just such "I Want to Go Home" moments, when it is so easy to say negative words and so hard to come up with positive distractions. Hopefully, these ideas will help you and your child make some of those necessary waits actually pleasant.

The ideas in this chapter include:

• Four games, requiring no equipment, that stimulate a kid's abilities to think, to wonder, and to observe: What If? People Watching, Add-a-Line Stories, and Fill-in-the-Rhyme

• Grocery Search, a game to amuse and teach your kid while you market

• Two paper-and-pencil activities: Unfolded Monster Drawings and Flip Book

• Whirling Button, a toy that a kid can keep in a pocket for tight-space emergencies

■ What If? ■

"What If?" is a game to stretch a child's imagination while distracting her from an earache or from a bad case of the fidgets. To get you started, what if . . .

• sidewalks were conveyor belts?
• it never rained?
• it were summer all the time?
• you were a bumblebee?
• everybody looked just the same?
• everybody lived in the city?
• everybody lived in the country?
• we didn't have electricity?
• worms had wings?
• dogs could talk?
• the school bus doesn't come?
• you had three wishes?
• you were on a desert isle and could have only three things?

Age Range: 3 and up, with help

What a Grown-up Is to Do

1. Ask your child a question that you do not have the answer to. There are no right or wrong answers.

2. If your child is stumped by your question, give a little help, like, "Well, I think if dogs could talk, then Fluffy would be saying to Dad right now, 'Please scratch my head just behind my left ear.' What else do you think Fluffy might say?"

Helpful Hints for Grown-ups

• The goal of this activity is to get your kid thinking productively and positively. Questions that encourage positive answers might be: "What if you see a kitten stuck up in a tree and you want to help it get down?" or "What if you have used up your allowance and you need to earn some money to buy a new toy?"

• Usually, "What Ifs" are best if they are *off* the subject of an immediate problem or tense situation. The point is to distract the child from what worries her (or you). Questions that don't help would be: "What if you have the worst earache the doctor has ever seen?" or "What if we're in such a hurry that we forget to buy the icing for your birthday cake?" or "What if Santa goes on a coffee break before it's your turn to talk to him?"

■ People Watching ■

When waiting at the train station or bus stop seems to take forever, simply watching other people can be an interesting activity. Paying attention to others means that kids in tight spaces are less inclined to pay attention to their own little woes.

Age Range: 4 and up, with help

What the Grown-up Is to Do

1. Teach your child the rules of people watching: No staring, no pointing, and no loud comments allowed! The trick is to watch people without letting them know that they are being watched.

2. To get your child started making observations, you might whisper, "I see a little boy in a green jacket. He is looking for something. He looks worried. I wonder why. Maybe he lost his spelling paper. What do you think?"

3. Make up a story together about the people you watch.

Helpful Hints for Grown-ups

People Watching is fun with a purpose. Its ultimate goal is to help kids observe others, to become sensitive to others' feelings, and to become aware that they themselves are important members of our one, great community.

However, some kids (and adults, too) watch people for a while and then make fun of them. Usually, they laugh because they are uncomfortable. If you find that your child is mean to others, belittles them, or makes unkind comments, it is important to find out why.

You may not want to find out why. After all, you don't want your kid to harbor negative feelings, and you certainly don't want to dwell on them. But the fact is that your kid does have negative feelings, because he's human.

So, rather than ending the People Watching activity by saying, "It isn't nice to laugh or to say mean things," seize the moment to have a little heart-to-heart chat with your kid.

Maybe he notices a child in a wheelchair, or a man covered with tattoos, or a very fat woman. Maybe he responds inappropriately because he observes differences in their abilities or looks that make him uncomfortable. What are his thoughts, perceptions, feelings? Is he afraid? Is he angry?

Give your kid the reassurance and information that he needs, so that he will grow to be not only a good people watcher, but also a good "people person"!

Learning Value

People Watching teaches a kid:

* to develop keen observation skills,
* to hypothesize about what may be happening or may be about to happen,
* to empathize with others, and
* to recognize and acknowledge his own feelings.

■ Add-a-Line Stories ■

Add-a-Line Stories are wonderful for any situation where your child feels antsy. Like the "What If?" activity (page 150), this one appeals to kids because it is a game you play together and because there are no right or wrong responses. In fact, the wackier the better!

Age Range: 3 and up, usually with help

What to Do

1. Take turns saying one line at a time to tell a story. The story doesn't have to have a plot, but often, in a crazy sort of way it will make sense.

2. Here's an example of how one might go:

> GROWN-UP: Let's tell an Add-a-Line Story. Here is a beginning: Once there was a beautiful duck. Now, you say what happens next.
>
> CHILD: The duck got in a spaceship and went straight up, up, up to the moon.
>
> GROWN-UP: The Man in the Moon was very glad to see the beautiful duck.
>
> CHILD: The duck said, "Quack, quack" to the Man in the Moon.
>
> GROWN-UP: The Man in the Moon said, "I hear you quacking very beautifully."
>
> CHILD: The duck said, "I like quacking."
>
> GROWN-UP: The Man in the Moon said, "Why do you quack?"

CHILD: The duck said, "Because I'm not afraid of anything, not even you, Mr. Moon!"

GROWN-UP: The Man in the Moon said, "I like quackers."

CHILD: The duck said, "Don't eat me!"

GROWN-UP: The Man in the Moon said, "Don't worry; I like quackers and cheese!"

CHILD: The duck said, "Oh, I do, too."

GROWN-UP: The Man in the Moon said, "Well, then, let's have a tea party."

CHILD: Yum, yum. The End.

Helpful Hint for Grown-ups

Try to let the kid steer the direction of the Add-a-Line Story. This is a perfect opportunity for you to be an active listener and to follow the kid's lead. You will learn a lot about your child's innermost thoughts and emotions.

■ Fill-in-the-Rhyme ■

This is another game that is good for any place or time when your kid is feeling cramped. As an activity that brings the old and the young together, it can't be beat. Grandparents enjoy it as much as kids, because it is satisfying to pass rhymes down through the generations.

Age Range: 4 and up, with a grown-up's participation

What to Do

1. One person begins a ditty with a catchy rhythmic beat, and leaves out the last word.

2. The next person's job is to fill in the blank with an appropriate rhyme.

3. Here are some examples:

> *I know a boy who likes to cook,*
> *And when he's done, we'll read a* _____*(book).*

> *Jiggedy, joggedy, jiggedy jig,*
> *A girl I know just loves to* _____*(dig).*
> *Jiggedy, joggedy, jiggedy jug,*
> *This girl just loves to kiss and* _____*(hug).*

> *Katie rides a scooter,*
> *And Charley rides a bike,*
> *Chelsea rides a big wheel,*
> *And Justin rides a* _____ *(trike).*

This is a Fill-in-the-Rhyme that my father used to sing and chant to my sister and me when we were small:

> *I've got two daughters*
> *And I think they're very cute.*
> *One is so pretty*
> *And the other is a* _____ *(beaut)!*

> *I've got two daughters*
> *And I think they're pretty great.*
> *One is eleven*
> *And the other one is* _____ *(eight).*

And here it is again, a generation later, revised to apply to my own little boys:

> *I've got two grandsons*
> *And I think they're pretty neat-o.*
> *One is a cricket*
> *And the other's a* _____ *(mosquito)!*

Variations

Do you like to make up rhymes to drop into songs? Try these:

"A-HUNTING WE WILL GO"

Oh, a-hunting we will go,
A-hunting we will go,
We'll catch a fox
And put him in a box
And then we'll let him go.

• Replace "fox" with other animals and think of a place to put each different animal. Examples are:

We'll catch a bear
And put him in your hair . . .

or We'll catch a raccoon
And put him in a balloon . . .

or We'll catch a snake
And put him in a cake . . .

or We'll catch a mouse
And put him in a house . . .

• Another old favorite is this camp song:

OH, YOU CAN'T GET TO HEAVEN

Oh, you can't get to heaven
On roller skates,
'Cause you'll roll right past
The Pearly Gates.

• Repeat the first line and replace the next three with rhymes like:

In this old car,
'Cause this old car
Can't go that far.

or   In Daddy's boat,
Cause Daddy's boat
Needs one more coat.

* And then there's:

"DOWN BY THE BAY"

Down by the bay,
Where the watermelons grow,
Back to my home,
I dare not go.
For if I do,
My mother will say,
"Did you ever see a cat (or, Did you ever see a cow)
Sitting in a Hat? (Saying bow-wow?)"
Down by the bay.

Helpful Hints for Grown-ups

It's perfectly all right for young children to suggest non-sense words to fill in the blanks. For example, instead of saying "A girl I know just loves to *dig*," a young child may respond with, "A girl I know just loves to *zig*."

Zig is a terrific rhyming word! Dig it!

■ Grocery Search ■

Going to the grocery store is no fun for most children, especially when they are stuck in the grocery cart kiddy seat. Try this simple activity to involve your child in the shopping. A boring experience becomes interesting when a kid feels needed and successful.

Age Range: 4 and up, with help

What You Will Need
Grocery coupons

What the Grown-up Is to Do
1. If your child is small enough to sit in the kiddy seat:
   Hand her a coupon for a food she likes, such as one for her favorite breakfast cereal.
   Push the cart slowly down the aisle where cereals are shelved.
   Let your child match the coupon to the box. Even kids who are too young to read letters are able to recognize pictures and symbols. That's how learning to read words begins!
2. If your bigger child doesn't fit into the kiddy seat:
   Give her 3 coupons at a time.
   Let her walk up and down the same aisle you're in, while she looks for grocery items to match the coupons.

Helpful Hints for Grown-ups
• Group the coupons so that similar items are together.
• Keep your child within sight at all times.

Variation
Next time you're at an art museum, go first to the gift shop and choose about six postcards of paintings or sculptures in the collection. Then, go on an Art Search. When you find a work of art to match the postcard, it will be an exciting discovery.

Learning Value
Grocery Search teaches:

• visual discrimination,
• word recognition, and
• how to be a smart consumer.

■ Unfolded Monster Drawings ■

Anytime you and your child are waiting, at a restaurant, for instance, you may enjoy this amusing activity. Once the kids get the hang of it, they can do it without your help—and they will, over and over again!

Age Range: 5 and up, with help at first

What You Will Need
Pencils
Paper

What the Grown-up Is to Do
1. Draw a monster's head near the top edge of a piece of paper. (Don't let the child peek.)
2. Pencil in 2 lines for a neck.
3. Fold the paper so that the head is hidden from the child's sight, but so the neck extends below the fold. The child will need to see the neck in order to attach a torso.
4. Hand the pencil and the folded paper to your child and say, "Now you draw the body and arms of the monster. I won't look. Then draw lines for where the legs should be, and fold the paper so I can see only the tops of the legs."
5. Give the kid plenty of time to draw the monster's body and arms. Remind him, if necessary, to indicate where you are supposed to put the legs when your turn comes.
6. Then you draw the legs, fold the paper, and give the paper to the child to add the feet.
7. Let the child have the pleasure of unfolding the paper.
8. Do it again, this time letting him start by drawing the head.

Variation
Make Unfolded Animal Drawings, or Unfolded House Drawings.

■ Flip Book ■

With your ever-ready paper and pencil, a child can make a mini-movie while waiting in the doctor's office. This is engrossing work for even the most anxious or bored kid.

Age Range: 8 and up

What You Will Need
A pad of paper or a small notebook
Pencil with an eraser

What to Do
1. Open the pad to the last page. In the lower left corner, draw a small, simple figure, such as:
a stick figure
a face
a ghost
a little car
the sun or the moon
2. Turn to the next-to-last page in the pad and draw a similar figure, a little more to the right.
3. Keep turning pages backward and drawing the same figure in slightly different positions.
4. When you have about 10 figures, close the pad. With your right thumb, ripple the pages that you have drawn on. See how your figure seems to move? That's how animated movies are made.

Helpful Hint for Grown-ups
Making a Flip Book requires good fine-motor skills and eye-hand coordination. By the time a child is in the third grade, she should have mastered her pencil grip and simple drawing

skills. Younger children will probably be frustrated by trying to make a Flip Book themselves, but they will love watching you make one and will enjoy playing with it.

■ Whirling Button ■

This button activity is a snap! Making it is easy for elementary-school-age kids. You can make it anywhere, play with it anywhere, and keep it tucked in your pocket for emergencies.

Age Range: 7 and up

What You Will Need
3' of string or dental floss
Large button with 2 holes (if your button has 4 holes, that's okay; just use 2 holes)

What to Do
1. Push the thread through one hole and then back through the other hole of the button.
2. Knot the ends of the string together.
3. Move the button to the middle of the string.

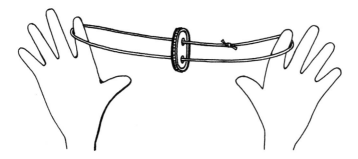

4. Put the button and string down on a table, and separate the string at both ends to make loops.

5. Stick your index fingers into the loops and pick up the Whirling Button.

6. Press your index fingers and thumbs together to keep a firm grip on the string.

7. Making circular movements with your wrists, whirl the button until the string is wound tightly.

8. Keeping your fingers in the loops, pull the string ends apart. The button will whirl as the string unwinds.

9. Do it again, making the string very tight and then pulling it very hard and fast. The button will make a humming sound.

10. Keep the Whirling Button in your pocket. It may come in handy soon, when you are in another tight space and want something fun to do.